The Paradox of Training

The Paradox of Training:

Making Progress out of Crisis

Denis Gleeson

OPEN UNIVERSITY PRESS
Milton Keynes • Philadelphia

Open University Press
12 Cofferidge Close
Stony Stratford
Milton Keynes MK11 1BY

and
242 Cherry Street
Philadelphia, PA 19106, USA

First Published 1989

British Library Cataloguing in Publication Data

Gleeson, Denis
  The paradox of training : making progress out of crisis.
  1. Great Britain. Adolescents, 16–19 years.
  Employment. Effects of vocational education
  I. Title
  331.3′4′0941

  ISBN 0–335–09529–1
  ISBN 0–335–09528–3 Pbk

Library of Congress Cataloging-in-Publication Data

Gleeson, Denis.
  The paradox of training : making progress out of crisis/by Dennis Gleeson.
        p. cm.
  Bibliography: p.
  Includes index.
  1. Vocational education--Great Britain. 2. Education and state-Great
  Britain. I. Title.
  LC1047.G7G53 1988
  370.11′3′0941--dc19   88-19686   CIP
  ISBN 0–335–09529–1   ISBN 0–335–09528–3 (pbk.)

Typeset by Burns & Smith, Derby
Printed in Great Britain by the Alden Press, Oxford

For E, C and A

Contents

Acknowledgements   ix

1 The Paradox of Training   1

2 Tripartism and the New F.E.   18

3 Life Skills Training and the Politics of Personal Effectiveness   43

4 Pre-vocational Education for a Change   58

5 Progression and Progressivism in TVEI   77

6 Training and Its Alternatives   103

Glossary of Terms   118
Bibliography   120
Name Index   128
Subject Index   130

Acknowledgements

Many of the arguments in this book span both 'old' and 'new' areas of my work over the years, including research on industrial training, further education and apprenticeship, through to issues associatedwith YTS, TVEI, B/TEC, CPVE and related pre-vocational initiatives. Thus, for those practitioners and researchers whose interests in pre-vocational education and training pre-dates the rise of the so called 'new' vocationalism, they may well recognize ways in which arguments in this book build on my earlier endeavours. For this reason I must express gratitude to my various collaborators, namely, Michael Erben, Michael Hopkins, George Mardle, Allen Maunders, Gordon Smith and Geoff Whitty, who in direct and indirect ways have influenced the ideas expressed here.

If there is such a thing as guilt by association, I must equally express gratitude to Basil Bernstein, Brian Davies and Michael Young who, in the late 1960s and early 1970s at the Institute of Education, London University, inspired my interest in the sociology of further education and training, but on whom no blame can rest. To colleagues past and present, in particular John Eggleston, Philip Robinson, George Mardle, Allen Maunders, Iolo Roberts, Trevor Siggers, Mervyn Taylor and Alastaire Campbell, and to all members of the Research and Evaluation Unit at the University of Keele, I owe much to their professionalism and example. Equally, this debt applies to students, teachers and advisers in neighbouring LEAs, schools and colleges, most notably in Staffordshire and Cheshire with whom I have worked closely over the years. I am also grateful to colleagues in NATFHE (General Studies Section), ALE and ATSS for their comments on earlier drafts of this book, and to Edwina Gleeson and Gladys Pye who, in their own exceptional ways, ensured that the project was completed.

Acknowledgement is due to Croom Helm, Routledge and Kegan Paul, Pergamon Press, the *Sociological Review*, the *Journal of Critical Social Policy* and *Educational Review*, for permission to use material that has appeared in different forms in various of their publications, but which has been substantially revised and updated here for the purposes of this book. I am also grateful to the *DES Statistical Bulletin* for allowing me to quote from their statistics and to ESRC and the University of Keele for their support in relation to various parts of this book.

Denis Gleeson

The Paradox of Training

This book analyses present-day vocational education and training policies as they affect contemporary schooling and further education. In particular, the book examines where young people fit into the ever changing arrangements of further education and training practice across the 14–19 age range. To date, much of what counts as vocational relevance in the curriculum has been government and employer led, but this book considers the issue from the angle of students and teachers – a constituency largely ignored in the shifting debate about what is vocationally worth while for young people. Instead of adopting a *pro* or *anti* stance, a position often favoured by recent commentators of the new vocationalism, this book critically explores the paradoxes and contradictions which characterize the various competing strands of government education and training policy. In so doing the intended and unintended consequences of such policy are explored, with particular reference to many of the less obvious signs of innovation and change emerging from the tensions involved.

There is, of course, no one paradox of training, there are many, perhaps the most interesting of which arise from the unintended outcomes of the best laid official plans. In identifying some of these, this book maintains that a clearer understanding of the contradictions associated with government training reforms may be gleaned, thereby informing a more coherent analysis of the *alternatives* needed to secure a comprehensive system of further education and training. On the surface this would seem an ambitious project given the way the ground rules of the new vocationalism, involving NTI, YTS, TVEI, CPVE, LAPP, B/TEC, NCVQ and other such weird abbreviations, have changed over the past decade.*

---

* See Glossary on page 118 for an explanation of these terms.

Yet in other respects there are signs that the frenetic momentum of training reform in the 14–19 age range has settled down, finding its expression within the conventional arrangements of mainstream education – though some critics maintain that it has simply been tacked on at the end. What the *Paradox of Training* seeks to do is examine such issues but with particular reference to the ways in which progress may arise from the contradictions involved.

In the past decade government policy has sought to alter the traditional arrangements of school and further education in favour of more vocationally oriented employer-led training initiatives. This book examines the response of school and further education to such initiatives across the 14–19 age range, including the introduction of schemes such as YTS, TVEI, B/TEC, CPVE and related pre-vocational courses. Such developments have not been without controversy. To some, current government training policy is conspiratorial in nature, reflecting little more than the government's desire to create a more compliant work force. To others, vocational reform in our schools and colleges is long overdue, reflecting a positive step toward furnishing a more relevant curriculum for the majority of school leavers. In examining such apparently contrasting views this book critically analyses both the intended and unintended consequences of vocational education and training policy. A principal argument is that, if the conspiratorial view would seem compelling, it is the actual *practice* of vocational initiatives, at school and college level, that is more interesting – not least in pointing up the very contradictions between education and work which they were originally designed to address. Thus, despite the centralist and often prescriptive thrust of MSC (or Training Agency as it is now known) and government training policy, including the Education Act (1988)* and the National Curriculum, at the local level a number of unintended innovations are now taking place. These include a broadening of the curriculum across the 14–19 age range, the introduction of more active learning programmes, closer links between school and college, and more student-centred approaches. Either way the question remains: what is the point of relevant vocational education when the possibilities of obtaining employment remain limited?

The paradox of training is not simply that there 'ain't no jobs', but that vocational training remains a crucial feature of preparation for a world in which work for many may not exist. As job prospects for school leavers become increasingly pessimistic, it is ironic that there is pressure on school and college to reflect the world of work through a variety of new vocational education and training reforms. Yet, if vocational realism has become the catchword of the 1980s, there can be little doubt that training without work does not make sense: it is a contradiction in terms. In view of this apparent

---

* Though written during the passage of GERBIL the book anticipates the Education Act itself and refers to it as such throughout.

contradiction, what useful purpose does further education or training serve in either equipping young people for the world of work or for the world of unemployment? It is to this central question that this book is addressed.

Neglected territory?

Until recently further education and training attracted little political or public interest, its technical and 'night school' image often being associated with apprenticeship and low status industrial employment. If in the late 1960s and early 1970s further education and training could be described as the 'Cinderella' of the education system, in the late 1980s it has come to occupy a central role in linking school and work. Two main factors explain why this is the case. First, the degree of decentralized development traditionally associated with F.E. has been increasingly brought under State control designed to incorporate F.E. within the broader context of government training policy. Second, successful government attempts to reshape school, F.E. and LEA budgets to make them more responsive to national requirements, including NCVQ, GRIST and the Education Act 1988, have increased the central power of government in delivering its training reforms at the local level. Thus, following on the New Training Initiative (1981) and the introduction of YTS (1981) and TVEI (1983), a number of important measures have radically altered pre-vocational education and training across the 14–18 range. In a relatively short space of time a number of influential policy documents – *Training for Jobs* (1984), *Better Schools* (1985) and *Working Together* (1986) – have extended the impetus of centralized government education and training reforms, culminating in the introduction of the National Curriculum.

Yet, despite their sudden arrival on the scene, YTS, TVEI, CPVE and related pre-vocational initiatives have their roots in a wider historical debate about the aims of education, not least regarding the ways further education and schooling should respond to industry's needs. In the past three decades, and culminating in the so-called Great Education Debate (1976–79), schools have been criticized for being anti-industry and for promoting academic values in the curriculum at the expense of relevant technical and vocational skills. Indeed, as Reeder (1981) maintains, the argument that entrepreneurial culture should find its expression in the curriculum is not new; it has its origins in nineteenth century conceptions of schooling and is part of a 'recurring debate' (see Wiener, 1981; McCulloch, 1987). Perhaps what is new is the timing and scale of government intervention in restructuring mainstream education in order to implement centrally conceived initiatives. In a period otherwise characterized by cut-back and retrenchment in the education system, YTS and TVEI constitute a novel, if not paradoxical, exception to the rule. With total government spending on further education and training earmarked at £13.5b[1] in the period 1986–87 to 1990–91, YTS, TVEI and a range of pre-vocational courses including adult Employment Training Initiative represent a distinct break with hitherto accepted models of curriculum development, and reflect a 'new' approach to the way in which central government sets the educational and training agenda at the local level.

Since the early 1970s, with rising youth unemployment, school and further education have been subjected to an extended period when the very ground rules of schooling have altered. The presence of the new 'sixth former' after ROSLA and the Newsom 'child', promoted thoughts about changing the curriculum and teaching methods and has resulted in a plethora of *relevant* pre-vocational courses in the 14–19 age range of which TVEI, CPVE and LAPP are but a few. At the centre of the most recent impetus for change could be seen the dramatic collapse of the youth labour market in the mid- to late-1970s. This collapse has meant that for many young people schools were no longer seen as the main transition or transmission point into a job at sixteen. Change in pupil destinations has paradoxically promoted greater awareness within educational circles of the inadequacies of market forces to regulate school to work transitions, and of the need to initiate widespread curricular innovation and reforms. As I have argued elsewhere (Gleeson, 1987) almost simultaneously a politically inspired debate about the purposes and practices of schooling has arisen. At one level, criticism has been directed at the apparent failure of school and F.E. to ensure a proper 'fit' between the vocational needs of young people and the requirements of the economy (Gleeson and Mardle, 1980). At another, critics argue that the current obsession with training is flawed, and obscures a more fundamental problem, namely that youth labour markets have collapsed. Either way, Dale (1985) maintains that the significance of YTS and TVEI relates to the prevailing crises which each were designed to address at the time.

Yet, if youth unemployment can be said to have generated a structural legitimacy crisis for mainstream education it has also, paradoxically, drawn attention to largely ignored contradictions in the relations between school, college and work (Roberts, 1984). At one level, this has unleashed negative forces designed to more functionally control schooling which have, in part, obscured the changes in capital which originally gave rise to that crisis. At another, it has drawn attention to those very changes and forces, thereby opening up certain possibilities for critical intervention and reconstruction. Without wishing to exaggerate the room for manoeuvre allowed by recent government inspired initiatives in education, it is important to recognize that central control is neither clear cut nor determined. Despite attempts by government to regulate the worst effects of youth unemployment via training, the inadequacies of its various schemes have increased public awareness of the sorts of question which vocational training has sought to repress – namely, what is the purpose of training without work? (Finn,

1987). The gaps and inconsistencies which surround this question have been opened up still further by the imposition of highly centralized schemes which, at the local level, often display progressive features, negotiated learning, active learning and experimental learning, and which presuppose a shift in the balance of power and control in the curriculum. In this respect the paradox of training is that the intended and unintended consequences of various training programmes do not functionally add up, revealing the contested rather than given nature of government training policy at the present time.

Thus, despite the apparent vocational bias evident in recent training initiatives, a number of quite unintended consequences have arisen, not least those which emphasize innovative elements associated with equal opportunities, multi-racial education and active learning. Pring (1985b) for example, has pointed to the ways in which TVEI and related pre-vocational initiatives have drawn attention to gaps in educational provision, and have forced a rethink about how young people are educated and trained. Yet in other respects this would seem inconsistent with the Conservative government's reasons for introducing training reforms in the first place, namely that schools and colleges were engendering anti-industrial attitudes among young people. Thus, if TVEI, YTS and related vocational schemes reflect a certain prescriptive restructuring of educational priorities around the 'needs' of industry, the progressive orientation of the curriculum which supports the new vocationalism is often at variance with such prescription. As Blackman (1987) has commented, much depends on who receives the progressive curriculum and to what ends such progressive education is to be directed. The danger, he maintains, is that integration and progressiveness will themselves become streamed concepts: 'both the able and less able students receiving a new integrated curriculum but within either an implicitly or an explicitly streamed system.'

Differentiation and change

Since their inception in schools and colleges in the early 1980s YTS and TVEI have been the object of much controversy. At one level, debate has centred on the way in which the MSC has sought to inject greater vocational realism into the curriculum. At another, perhaps more problematic level, central government control in the running of schools and colleges, notably via MSC and the Education Act (1988), has drawn attention to wider political changes in policy and decision making processes in education. Up to the late 1970s most HMI and DES reports focused upon the broad-based nature of the curriculum and, despite the growing influence of the Black Paper Writers and the New Right, argued for 'curricular balance' invoking liberal humanist conceptions of education.

Influenced by the Ruskin Speech (Callaghan, 1976), FEU's *ABC* (1979) and MSC's *A New Training Initiative* (1981), the 'vocationalist' argument can be seen to have become more insistent and influential. From the early 1980s the Conservative government and the MSC have sought to alter awareness about changes in the labour market via schooling. According to Youthaid (1984) the Conservative government views the MSC as a means of introducing market-place realities into the world of education, and has used the 'crisis' of unemployment and schooling to secure political control of education and training. Perhaps, not surprisingly, vocational realism has become, in certain quarters, the order of the day with *enterprise culture* as its focal point.

Following on the so-called Great Education Debate (1976–79) the MSC (as of October 1988 this title has again been changed and is now referred to as The Training Agency) has been at the forefront of government training policy, directly intervening in curriculum development, LEA policy and links between school, further education and work. Moreover, as a major agent of the Department of Employment, the MSC has bypassed conventional democratic channels and now deals direct with LEAs, schools and colleges. This model, supporters maintain, has sped up the process of change in the period 1981–88, thereby allowing innovation and resources to percolate through to the grass roots level more effectively. This break with the previous involvement of the DES in curriculum development and a corresponding move towards centralism might be seen within educational circles as a truly innovative, although not necessarily welcome, one (Gleeson and Maunders, 1985). On the more positive side it is acknowledged that MSC involvement has brought TVEI about in rapid time compared with, for example, the Certificate of Pre-vocational Education (CPVE), which was developed via the more established DES/LEA route. In this respect it is not simply the amount of resources allocated by central government that is important, but also the degree and means of their control. Specifically, it is to the MSC and government that LEAs have had to make a *contractual* commitment to deliver YTS and TVEI. This represents a radical departure from conventional modes of curricular delivery established over time via unwieldy democratic channels between schools, colleges, LEAs, DES, unions, Schools Council (now disbanded) and so forth. Moreover, with the introduction of the National Curriculum this so-called 'radical departure' has now become institutionalized, reflecting a growing centralist *rapprochement* between the DES, Training Commission and the Department of Employment.

For the purpose of this book what remains less than clear is the part non-advanced F.E. (NAFE) and vocational schooling is likely to play within the more centralized arrangements of government education and training policy. At the moment F.E. and training is in the melting pot, between its traditional localized relationship with the labour market and the newer, more centralized, requirements of national training policy (NTI) which have come to impinge upon it. The same is true, of course, of schooling in general, notably in relation to the initiation and extension of TVEI and the constraints imposed by the Education Act and National Curriculum. In other respects, however, Further Education is no longer a peripheral part of mainstream education catering simply for the needs of those already *in* employment – in many respects it has become more school focused, almost an adjunct to schooling itself. Perhaps, not surprisingly, the collapse of the youth labour market and subsequent patterns of unemployment have radically altered traditional conceptions of school, college and work transition, and has highlighted the role F.E. and training is likely to play. Thus, in contrast with previous decades when only a minority of school leavers participated in further education and training, increasing numbers now spend significant amounts of time in F.E., and in work-related, pre-vocational, link courses, vocational preparation and other schemes. Enrolments in NAFE, for example, including YTS, rose from 1,619,000 in 1984 to 1,659,000 in 1985, and to 1,732,000 in 1986. Students enrolled in F.E. establishments as part of their YTS schemes numbered 32,000 in 1982, 104,000 in 1983, 114,000 in 1984, 115,000 in 1985 and 118,000 in 1986. In other respects the number of students aged 16–18 on full-time and sandwich courses increased by 1% to 305,000 in 1985 and to 595,000 in 1986. Total enrolments by the 16–18 age group, which had remained constant at 691,000 for two years, declined marginally to 688,000 in 1985 and 1986, although participation rates increased (DES, 1986). In relation to special needs, a recent DES (1987) survey indicates that such students were to be found on all types of mainstream course, including those in Higher Education.[2] However, special courses were mainly provided by colleges with a high proportion of students in NAFE and tertiary colleges. Looking at YTS as a separate category, there were in August 1987 an estimated 398,000 trainees on YTS courses, 142,000 of whom were in their second year of training.[3]

On current forecasts the population aged 19–24 is projected to fall from a peak in 1986 to a low point in 1999. According to recent DES projections (DES, 1988) the effects of this on NAFE are likely to be offset by rising levels of student participation, particularly in the range of new courses accredited through the National Council for Vocational Qualifications (NCVQ) (see Table 1). In addition what is noticeable is the enrolment of students aged 25 and over on NAFE courses. These numbers have dramatically increased from 440,000 in 1980 to nearly 750,000 in 1986. Moreover, enrolments are projected to rise throughout the period 1986–94 to between 890,000 and 970,000 students, mainly on part-time and evening courses. It is also partly in anticipation of such rising demand among 20–25 year olds that the Conservative government recently introduced its Adult Employment Training Programme (1988), aspects of which are discussed in the chapters which follow.

If such figures indicate only an imprecise picture of F.E.'s involvement

Table 1 Projected numbers of students in maintained colleges studying on non-advanced courses: England 1986–2000

NAFE enrolments in England – home and EC students in maintained colleges – 1980–2000

		1980	1986	1990	1994 (trough)	Thousands 2000
Full-time and sandwich	Low	275	322	282	255	285
	High			290	273	324
Part-time	Low	1,049	1,279	1,321	1,316	1,397
	High			1,365	1,423	1,617
YTS (in colleges) – all modes		8	119	153	131	146
All enrolments	Low	1,331	1,720	1,756	1,702	1,828
	High			1,808	1,827	2,088
Full-time equivalent enrolments	Low	457	537	510	471	517
	High			524	502	584

NAFE age participation rates and enrolments in England by age – 1980–2000 – home and EC students in maintained colleges

		1980	1986	1990	1994 (trough)	Thousands (enrolments) 2000
Students aged between 16 and 18 years old						
Age participation rate (per cent)	Low	26.8	29.7	31.5	32.2	32.9
	High			32.2	33.9	36.3
All enrolments	Low	621	647	599	514	578
	High			612	542	638
Full-time equivalent enrolments	Low	314	347	310	271	310
	High			318	287	345
Students aged between 19 and 24 years old						
Age participation rate (per cent)	Low	6.5	6.9	7.7	7.7	8.0
	High			7.8	8.2	8.9
All enrolments	Low	271	325	341	301	271
	High			349	318	300
Full-time equivalent enrolments	Low	75	83	83	72	67
	High			85	76	73
Students aged 25 years old or more						
Age participation rate (per cent)	Low	1.5	2.4	2.6	2.8	3.0
	High			2.7	3.0	3.5

All enrolments	Low	440	748	816	887	978
	High			847	967	1,149
Full-time equivalent	Low	69	107	117	127	141
enrolments	High			121	139	166

(Adapted from DES (1988) *Projected Numbers of Students in Maintained Colleges Studying on Non-Advanced Courses: England: 1986–2000*, Statistics Branch)

with YTS (estimates indicate 150,000 trainees in 1988–89), there can be little doubt about the changing patterns of student participation in NAFE projected over the next decade. In addition to providing trade training, professional and academic courses, F.E. offers training opportunities to a wide cross-section of school leavers, including the employed, the unemployed and those undertaking pre-vocational courses. Following on the recent expansion of vocational and pre-vocational courses including TVEI, B/TEC, CPVE, City and Guilds and RSA, and closer liaison with YTS and schools, F.E. now accommodates a more heterogeneous student population than hitherto.[4] If to some this celebrates a major breakthrough in opening up F.E. as an alternative route 'for all' (Crowther, 1959), others have argued that F.E. has simply become a substitute for employment, reinforcing existing patterns of social inequalities (Brown and Ashton, 1987). Thus, despite the increasing levels of student participation in NAFE by age, class, race and gender, the eventual position of young people in the labour market may have changed very little.

Perhaps the central paradox of training policy is the simultaneous emergence of two apparently conflicting features. On the one hand, it reflects strong central control which has generated the detailed intervention of government, MSC and employer influence right down to the level of the classroom (Harland, 1987). On the other, schemes such as YTS, TVEI and others support local initiatives at the school and college level which, in many instances, are highly experimental and creative. In various ways, YTS, TVEI, CPVE and related vocational programmes have evolved to accommodate numerous 'progressive' teaching approaches drawn from the 1960s which themselves were the subject of much criticism at the time. Since 1984, emphasis on enrichment of the curriculum, active teaching methods and assessment based upon learning by doing, problem solving and practical experience, has become noticeable. Moreover, by linking TVEI with the delivery of the GCSE and the National Curriculum these objectives have become more commonplace. As various commentators have recently noted, there are positive features associated with the new vocationalism, such as new forms of assessment, profiling and records of achievement, development of new teaching styles, an integrated curriculum approach and the new pedagogic relations between teacher and student. Blackman (1987) has, for example, argued that the radical case for TVEI rests on three educational proposals:

. . . first, an integrated curriculum against a collection of separate subjects; second, pupil assessment and evaluation such as profiling against formal external examination and third, the new pedagogy of experiential learning and problem solving against traditional or academic learning.

Predictably, however, many of the principles to which Blackman refers find themselves in conflict with the guidelines laid down in the National Curriculum, reflecting a widening gap between traditional subject teaching and active learning approaches. If such duality mirrors deeper historical divisions and contradictions in education, it also finds its expression in recent government education and training policy itself. Thus, the idea that the current range of reforms on offer constitute a coherent package of agreed measures is illusory. Attempts to provide vocational training with a higher profile alongside academic and mainstream curriculum has, for example, floundered between two competing strands of government thinking – between those who believe in *enterprise* (the Lord Young Group) and those who believe in *standards* (the Hillgate Group). TVEI, for example, launched as a prototype to deliver more active ways of learning, new approaches to teaching strategies, problem solving and work experience out of school, has found itself in conflict with the National Curriculum, which makes little provision for integrated methods of teaching and learning. A principal aim of TVEI is that it should open up new opportunities for students across the ability range by interlinking vocational, academic and general knowledge in more relevant and applied ways. Indeed, the government White Paper *Better Schools* (1985) was so impressed with the achievements of TVEI that it advocated it as a prototype for future educational reform. Yet in the relatively short period between 1985 and 1988, the influential Hillgate Group, a right-wing pressure group with antecedents in the Black Papers, successfully fought a rearguard action within Conservative ranks to protect academic subjects against the spread of TVEI and related enterprise approaches, including GCSE and active learning approaches in the curriculum. One consequence of this is that, on the one hand, government has given weight and funding to a curriculum which emphasizes skills and areas of experience which cross subject boundaries, and involve cross-curricular projects and team work. On the other, it has thrown its support behind right-wing traditionalists whose main desire is to return to separate, clearly defined subjects backed up by testing and didactic teaching methods. Commenting on the influence of the Hillgate Group a *TES* editorial recently observed: 'They seem to have won hands down'. The editorial commented that in the early discussion of the National Curriculum, the plight of Latin got much more attention than that of economics, political literacy, business studies, home economics, politics, careers and information technology. Following on from this, the rather prescriptive models of testing envisaged in the Education Act (1988) are likely to severely restrict developments in active learning in schools and colleges. As Jamieson and Watts (1987) have observed, some of the strongest sources of active learning have been work experience, work shadowing, residential courses, mini enterprises, Outward Bound courses and community based activities – all areas of the curriculum provided with little or no recognition within the confines of the National Curricular Guidelines.

Realism and idealism

Whether or not in practice progressive approaches associated with the new vocationalism actually contradict or complement government intentions, there can be little doubt that vocational education and training across the 14–19 age range is currently experiencing a significant change in direction. With the decline in manufacturing industry the traditional ethos of craft education has shifted away from job training and 'making things', to schemes designed to anticipate new jobs in the labour market. In many respects, the government's New Training Initiative (NTI, 1981) has administered the last rites to the traditional apprenticeship system, replacing it with an *enterprise* model of training based on entrepreneurial rather than industrial values. Thus, an important aim of the new vocationalism is to encourage individualism and greater economic awareness in young people of the reality of market forces, thereby making them less dependent on employers and the State for their livelihoods. From this viewpoint further education and training is not simply something which prepares trainees for existing jobs in the labour market but it is also part and parcel of the job creation process itself.

Unfortunately, such an idealization of how market forces operate in everyday life is purely mythological. In practice school and F.E. are neither so autonomous nor so innovative as this would seem to imply. Viewed more sceptically, time served training has been replaced by serving time on government schemes with little indication that the skills learned have any direct bearing on future employment opportunities or on the market itself. For many the syndrome of chronic job changing in the 1960s has simply been replaced by chronic scheme changing in the 1980s (Raffe, 1983b; Roberts, 1984). If student participation rates in further education and training would seem to have dramatically increased, considerable ambiguity remains about how far F.E. and training represent an alternative route or a second choice for those students traditionally denied access to its ranks, but now included via MSC provision.

Recent evidence indicates that far from challenging inequalities in training and work, F.E. reinforces various tripartite divisions separating the unemployed 'trainees' from the 'students' studying academic, technical and professional courses (Gleeson, 1983; Green, 1986). A significant factor in the new tripartism is the way in which MSC, DHSS,

DES and Further Education have become locked into the 'poverty trap', defining the unemployed as an underclass via training. By withdrawing benefits from those unwilling to undertake training a 'new' generation of conscript trainees and *refuseniks* has been produced. Whether training of the poor will, in Crowther's (1959) terms, '. . . help young people to find their way in the world . . .' remains to be seen. The likelihood is, however, that conscripts to training will neither identify with nor benefit from provision based on compulsion. The glum scenario is again one of ROSLA with all the attendant problems associated with alienation, boredom and discipline. From this perspective, training is not 'really useful knowledge', but something imposed from above which has only tenuous vocational relevance to either individual or employer, and contributes little to productive endeavour.

Thus, despite appearances there remains deep confusion in government thinking about the role vocational education and training is expected to play. Should training policy respond to problems in the labour market (training as a substitute for employment) or should it remedy skill shortages as they arise (training for employment)? Within its present remit, YTS, for example, represents something of a jack of all trades and master of none, responding neither to the crisis of mass youth unemployment nor to the crisis of skill shortage. In the circumstances, it is perhaps not surprising that government chooses other reference points than crisis to legitimate its vocational education and training reforms. In this respect, spurious international comparison, technological change and the conservatism of schooling itself have all been cited as more convenient ideological reasons for the necessity for reform. Much has been made, for example, of the kind of statistics which indicate how far Britain has fallen behind its competitors in the international league tables (see Prais, 1981):

Percentage of 16 to 18-year-olds in schools and training 1981

| | Full-time | | Part-time | |
	School	Training	(excl. YOP)	Total
Germany	31	14	40	85
USA	65	14	–	79
Japan	58	11	3	72
France	33	25	8	66
Italy	16	31	18	65
Britain	18	14	25	57

The nature of such international poor performance was documented in the Conservative government's policy statement, *A New Training Initiative*

(NTI, 1981a), which outlined the need to restructure vocational education and training across the 14–19 age range in favour of employer-led initiatives. According to Taylor (1988) the international comparison is made worse by the high degree of skill now demanded by the modern job market. In his view;

> As many as seventy per cent of the work force will soon be knowledge workers, reversing the situation of fifty years ago, when seventy per cent of workers were in manual, unskilled jobs. Brain is replacing brawn as a condition of employment. It is really not surprising that so many of our 16 year old leavers cannot find jobs. They have not learned the skills necessary for modern jobs.

There is, however, little evidence that widespread youth unemployment can be explained in this way. Such an argument represents little more than a convenient ideological rationale for government policy, particularly in relation to the introduction of City Technology Colleges (CTCs), in which Taylor has an interest. The number and type of jobs to which Taylor refers are few and far between, supporting the view that even if a majority of young people were to acquire high skill levels, there would not necessarily be the available jobs for them to go to. In reality, it is recession and lack of investment, rather than technology alone, which account for de-skilling and unemployment among the young. Providing young people with relevant skills, important as this may be, is not *the* answer: instead, employment policies alongside training reforms are more likely to have a long-term effect both on skill shortages and unemployment levels.

In examining these and related questions various commentators have noted a basic contradiction in much current thinking about how to improve the quality of training via government initiatives: namely, no questions are asked about the nature of work itself. According to Roberts (1984) even if full employment could be achieved tomorrow, the basic problem of how to make certain types of work less tedious, boring and dangerous would remain. Elsewhere, Tipton (1983) has argued that neither instrumental nor normative approaches to training, in their existing form, are likely to achieve any significant changes. It is, therefore, necessary to look more closely at the question of the control of work, its design, structure, organization and distribution alongside, rather than separate from, training programmes. At present the current obsession with training obscures any realization of achieving a closer fit between education and industry, mainly because work itself has been left out of the equation. According to Tipton (1983): 'If educationalists and trainers feel understandably squeamish about becoming involved in "narrow" training . . . then the solution is to combine policies for training with policies for work design.'

In seeking to get to grips with such issues *The Paradox of Training* takes a critical look at contemporary further education and training policy and in so doing advances a number of alternatives. Chapter two deals with the central role which further education now occupies in government training policy and examines the extent to which F.E. has become a substitute rather than a 'provider' of employment. Following on from this, the various consequences of F.E. practice on the lives and prospects of young people are considered with particular reference to the effects of recent legislation, in particular The New Training Initiative (NTI, 1981), Training for Jobs (1984) and the Education Act (1988). Two interrelated aspects of such legislation are addressed throughout the book. The first concerns the changing patterns of student participation in F.E. and training and the restructuring of youth opportunities via various *tripartite* divisions in the 'New F.E.'. The second concerns the broader context in which Conservative political and economic thinking finds its expression in the curriculum and organization of further education and schooling, thereby shaping the wider links between training and employment. This theme is taken up in chapter three which analyses the part played by 'social and life skills' in the further education and training process and, in particular, considers its political consequences in the light of recent attempts to restructure attitudes among the work force. Chapters four and five look at the recent phenomenon of pre-vocational education and its progressive effects (or not, as the case may be) on the changing structure of further education and training across the 14–19 age range. Chapter four deals rather more specifically with the potential challenge posed to mainstream F.E. by integrated pre-vocational and skills-based approaches associated with CPVE, B/TEC and related courses. Following on, chapter five considers the inroads made by TVEI on post-16 developments, in particular the links between school, college and work. Until recently TVEI was viewed very much as a school-based phenomenon, with little attention paid to the issue of progression at the post-16 level: it is to this neglected aspect of the present debate about TVEI that chapter five is addressed. In conclusion, chapter six examines various alternatives to the present scenario of training, in particular those advocating a more comprehensive view of further education and training, linked with programmes and policies for career advancement, access, job design and work. In so doing, *The Paradox of Training* seeks to provide a critical and constructive, as well as optimistic, insight into the ways in which students and teachers can take a more active part in the *process* of further education and training.

Notes

1. Despite major cuts to the MSC's budget, it remains by far one of the nation's biggest spenders, as the figures given in the table on p. 15 indicate:

Estimated MSC expenditure at cash prices

	1986–87	1987–88	1988–89	1989–90	1990–91
	£m	£m	£m	£m	£m
Youth Training Scheme	940.2	1,115.5	1,227.7	1,233.7	1,264.5
Community Industry Scheme	25.0	26.5	27.3	28.0	28.7
Adult and Occupational Training	317.1	489.5	541.9	555.8	569.7
Community Programme	1,068.0	1,071.0	1,174.1	1,205.4	1,235.6
Voluntary Projects Programme	14.5	12.9	12.7	13.0	13.3
Employment Rehabilitation	18.6	25.4	23.4	23.4	25.4
Non Advanced Further Education	112.7	115.4	118.3	121.2	124.2
Technical & Vocational Education Initiative	72.0	60.4	83.8	109.5	112.2
STEPS	5.0				
General employment services	120.3				
Restart	49.9				
Sheltered employment	83.2	These services were transferred			
Enterprise Allowance Scheme	150.3	to the Department of Employment			
Geographical Mobility	3.4	in Autumn 1987.			
Other employment services	16.9				
Professional and Executive Recruitment	0.5				
TOTAL PROGRAMMES	2,998.1	2,916.6	3,209.2	3,290.0	3,372.2
Skills Training Agency	−4.7	−5.9	−6.2	−5.4	−5.5
Support Services	39.0	39.7	39.6	39.4	40.4
TOTAL MSC	3,032.4	2,950.4	3,242.6	3,324.0	3,407.1

(Adapted from *Times Educational Supplement*, 25.12.87)

2. Estimated numbers of students with special educational needs

Type of course	Estimated number of students
Special Courses	
Link	12,500
Outreach	13,400
Specifically Provided Courses	
Part-time	6,100
Full-time	4,500
YTS	3,600
Mainstream Courses	3,400
All special needs students	43,500

Source: DES (1987, July) Statistical Bulletin: *Students in Further Education in England with Special Educational Needs*

3. Of these 95% were white, 57% male with less than 5% of the total from Black/African/Caribbean descent.

4. Further Educational enrolments: November

England   thousands

	1970	1975	1980	1984	1985	1986	Change 1985–1986 No	Per cent
F.E. Establishments								
Full-time & sandwich								
Men	192	231	235	278	280	288	+8	3
Women	171	231	248	297	302	307	+5	2
Total	363	462	483	575	582	595	+13	2
Part-time day Release								
Men	504	419	417	334	328	328	+0	0
Women	94	94	106	137	142	152	+10	7
Total	5987	514	523	472	470	480	+10	2
Other								
Men	26	45	53	110	113	123	+10	9
Women	92	153	124	188	205	220	+15	7
Total	118	198	177	298	318	343	+25	8
Evening only								
Men	325	310	244	288	290	305	+15	5
Women	391	467	372	396	427	459	+33	8
Total	716	776	616	685	717	764	+47	7
All part-time								
Men	855	774	715	733	730	756	+25	3
Women	577	715	602	721	774	831	+58	7
Total	1432	1488	1317	1454	1505	1587	+83	6
All courses in F.E. Establishments	1795	1950	1800	2029	2087	2182	+95	5
Adult Education Centres								
Men	434	580	475	390	384	397	+13	3
Women	886	1267	1068	1010	1034	1058	+24	2
Total	1320	1847	1543	1400	1418	1455	+37	3
All further education	3115	3797	3344	3429	3505	3637	+132	4

Students on Manpower Services Commission Schemes: November

England   thousands

	1980	1981	1982	1983	1984	1985	1986	Change 1985–1986 No	Per Cent
Youth Training Scheme									
16 year olds:									
Full-time and sandwich	3	5	16	22	16	17	14	−3	−19
Part-time day:									
– Released	2	3	4	50	66	66	62	−4	−6
– Other	1	4	5	14	12	11	9	−2	−19
Evening only	0	0	0	0	1	1	1	+0	44
Total	6	12	25	87	95	95	87	−9	−9
17 year olds:									
Full-time and sandwich	1	2	3	3	3	3	3	+0	14
Part-time day:									
– Released	0	1	2	10	12	13	22	+9	73
– Other	0	2	2	3	2	2	3	+1	49
Evening only	0	0	0	0	0	0	0	+0	137
Total	2	4	7	16	17	18	29	+11	62
16–18 year olds:									
Full-time and sandwich	4	8	20	26	19	20	18	−3	−14
Part-time day:									
– Released	2	5	6	60	79	80	86	+6	7
– Other	2	6	6	17	15	14	13	−1	−8
Evening only	0	0	0	0	1	1	2	+1	57
Total	8	18	32	104	114	115	118	+3	2
Other MSC	17	16	20	15	16	17	33	+16	93
All MSC sponsored students	25	34	52	119	130	132	152	+21	16

Source: DES (1987) Statistics of Further Education Students in England. Statistical Bulletin 13/87, November, 1987.

Tripartism
and the New F.E.

2

In the past decade the nature of further education and training has changed dramatically. If in the 1950s and 1960s further education was considered a sleepy backwater of the educational system, much has happened in the late 1970s and 1980s. Yet until recently the further education activities of 16–19 year olds remained a neglected area of enquiry, F.E.'s voluntaristic and entrepreneurial character perhaps reflecting the low status image traditionally associated with further education. With a few notable exceptions (Venables, 1967; Robinson, 1968; Tipton, 1973; Burgess, 1977; Cantor and Roberts, 1974) research in the sociology of education has tended to focus on school-based issues with little or no attention paid to the activities of industrial trainers and students. In addition to a prevailing lack of interest about vocational matters, the 'tech' or night school image of F.E. held little attraction for educationists in the 1960s, whose interests and experiences were mainly at the school level.

More recently, however, the legacy of youth unemployment and the rise of the MSC have ensured that the debate about further education and training is unlikely to remain the same. Once considered a peripheral area of concern, F.E. has now entered the forefront of political and educational debate. Since publication of the Crowther Report (1959) much has happened to the non-advanced sector of F.E. to bring it in line with mainstream educational developments and to redefine its role within broader tertiary principles. At the same time, however, the traditional degree of decentralized development enjoyed by F.E. has been increasingly brought under central control by government measures designed to incorporate NAFE within the wider context of State Training Policies.

The 'New F.E.'

The term 'New F.E.' refers to a wide range of pre-vocational, academic, professional and training courses, including adult and access courses which, from the late 1970s on, were designed to meet the vocational needs of a heterogeneous clientele. In contrast with the predominantly male day release craft intake of the 1950s and 1960s, the new F.E. appeals to a broad catchment of students including the employed, unemployed, and vocationally uncommitted.[1] Consequently, F.E. no longer caters solely for the needs of day release apprentices or those returning to take GCSE re-sits, although this provision remains an essential feature of the F.E. mandate. Instead, the 'New F.E.' has become more complex, incorporating students whose education and training horizons span almost the entire occupational structure. If, in the past, access to F.E. was principally determined by being *in* employment, or in such high status employment that it warranted employers releasing young people to college, that legacy has significantly altered. Male dominance of F.E., both in terms of staff and students, has altered dramatically, with noticeable improvements in student participation levels by age, class, race and gender.[2] Alongside this, the character and ethos of F.E. has correspondingly altered necessitating a rethink of the very aims and purposes of F.E. as it broadens its appeal to those previously denied access to its ranks.

Dramatic changes in the labour market, and subsequent patterns of youth unemployment and government training policies, have radically affected traditional conceptions of F.E. and training in the past decade. In addition to the conventional range of courses which it offers, F.E. is now strategically linked with national initiatives including NCVQ, YTS, TVEI, CPVE, B/TEC and the government's Training Employment Programme (ATP) (1988), which demand a rethink in the way in which F.E. structures its priorities at both local and national levels. Thus in many respects F.E. has absorbed change faster than any other area of the education system, providing a diverse range of courses to meet the needs of those in, out and anticipating employment. If, at one level, F.E. fulfils an important occupational role in providing skills for those entering specific types of occupation including nursing, business, social services, trade, industry and commerce, at another level it caters for those undertaking a variety of academic, professional and training schemes, including those who have not decided on a particular occupation and have enrolled on CPVE and related pre-vocational courses.

If, up to the mid 1970s, the vast majority of young people left school and went straight into employment or unemployment with little or no access to further education or training, that situation has now radically altered. Less than a decade later tertiary education has come to occupy a strategic role in opening up a wide range of youth and adult training and employment opportunities, designed to replace those eroded by recession, unemployment and the decline of the traditional apprenticeship system. There is, of course, the danger here of romanticizing what went before, in terms of an era when there was supposedly *training for real jobs*. Despite relatively full employment in the 1960s, however, fewer than 10% of school leavers had access to further education, training or skilled work. Thus, in comparison with the 'Old F.E.', the 'New F.E.' has in many ways come full circle – offering education and training courses to a broader audience hitherto denied access to its ranks.

From this perspective, it is clear that contemporary F.E. is no longer that narrow backwater of the education system it was once considered to be: increasing numbers of young people in the 16–19 age range spend significant amounts of time at college on a full- or part-time basis (DES, 1988). Many of the courses they now take are linked via school experience, including B/TEC foundation courses, City and Guilds, RSA, TVEI, LAPP and other pre-vocational programmes previously studied in the 14–16 age range. Following on such progression, courses at college span a broad spectrum, including GCSEs, 'A' levels, YTS, B/TEC First and National courses, CPVE and a wide range of professional and trade training courses relating to plumbing, surveying, catering, hairdressing, gas fitting, sport, leisure and recreation studies, and so forth. Thus, as further education has gradually made the transition from providing vocational training to those previously in employment to those out of work, the link between F.E. and (un)employment is now keenly debated. Not only has the mass extension of further education 'to all' stimulated new interest in the role of central government in regulating this link, but it has also generated wider public awareness about the relationship between F.E., school and work. Perhaps, not surprisingly, the 'new' F.E. has drawn attention to two hitherto neglected areas. The first concerns the changing patterns of student participation in F.E. in terms of race, class and gender, and the effect this has on 'who gets what' from training and F.E. Supporters of the new F.E. point to the comprehensive nature of its provision, referring to the way in which it offers 'second chance' and 'alternative opportunities' to those previously denied them (Cantor and Roberts, 1974; 1987; Bristow, 1976). The second area is, however, more problematic and concerns the ways in which government training policy has shaped F.E., in particular via the funding, control and accreditation of employer-led courses linked with MSC and NCVQ involvement.

At the moment F.E. is at the crossroads between its voluntaristic tradition and the newer compulsory elements that have come to challenge it. If, in 1968, the non-advanced sector of F.E. could be described as 'uncharted territory' (Robinson, 1968), this sector has now taken on a more systematic appearance. Paradoxically, the rise of youth unemployment has not only initiated far-reaching reforms, it has also bred fresh life into many of Crowther's original proposals notably in relation to the extension of F.E. 'for all'. If, however, Crowther's vision of the future would seem to have been realized, considerable ambiguity exists about how far F.E. and training represent an 'alternative route' or 'second chance' for those school leavers who traditionally went straight into work, but are now included through MSC and other forms of provision.

MSC, F.E. and the labour market

During a period in which government has reduced support for publicly-owned industry and pursued an uncompromising policy of privatization, training policy remains a conspicuous exception. As spending on advanced and non-advanced further education and training tops a staggering £3½b in 1988–89, a watershed in training policy has been reached whereby the state has now taken over from employers responsibility for training (Ryan, 1984). At a time when the efficiency of public sector enterprise is viewed with considerable scepticism, it is ironic that government policy should effectively nationalize training, thereby effectively removing responsibility for it from employers and placing it in the hands of the Civil Service. It should be recognized, however, that the Conservative government's New Training Initiative launched in 1981 does not simply represent a response to unemployment but is also designed to alter relations in the work-place in favour of employers (Fairley and Grahl, 1983). From this viewpoint, training has a closer relationship with private enterprise than might first appear; it also represents an important political mechanism through which labour is made ready and available for work even if such work does not exist.

Despite the recent controversy surrounding the way in which the MSC 'bought its way' into F.E. (Moos, 1984), its entry has been achieved relatively easily. If at one level this can simply be explained in terms of cash inputs, at another many educationalists, trade unionists and others welcomed MSC intervention as a progressive means of extending training provision to school leavers traditionally denied access to its ranks. Rising youth unemployment and the slow response of the DES in the mid-1970s prompted some commentators to view MSC overtures in a reformist light (Hayes, 1983; Watts, 1983). Moreover, attempts to initiate training measures such as YOP served only to illustrate the inadequacies of existing training provision and to legitimate the further extension of mass training as a good thing. However, at this time pragmatism and reformism also combined to enable colleges to maintain levels of student intake threatened by the collapse of local labour markets. In this respect LEAs and colleges were not 'innocent' parties in the market place negotiations that took place in the 1970s, wherein the flexibility of the points system allowed cash and provision to change hands.

Thus, the way in which private enterprise finds its expression in the arrangements of further education is not a new phenomenon. Indeed, the ethos of contemporary F.E. is rooted in its voluntaristic and entrepreneurial traditions, which have for long been associated with the fortunes of the local labour market. Unlike mass schooling, F.E. has taken a highly individualistic path, its survival depending very much on the patronage of local industry, and the ability of individual colleges to attract greater student numbers. As Tipton (1973) and Gleeson and Mardle (1980) have noted, the points system alone has ensured that many colleges remain in a perpetual state of flux, since they are constantly called upon to redefine their courses to attract new customers. This has ensured not only that the colleges operate on the basis of market forces, but also that they seek to manipulate the points system to ensure expansion and growth. Consequently, the emerging pattern of F.E. provision since the post-war period has been patchy and has come to depend on a points system firmly anchored to the production forecasts of local industry. Perhaps, not surprisingly, the development of those staple forms of provision that fall within the compass of F.E. have traditionally tended to be both parochial and chauvinistic, catering mainly for the needs of young male apprentice workers.

With the decline in demand for industrial craft work (manufacturing, shipbuilding, steel and so forth) in the 1960s and 1970s, F.E. was compelled to compensate for its loss in student intake by recruiting from a flourishing tertiary and service sector. The erratic pattern of industrial and corporate development in the 1960s, strange as it may now seem, led to demand for 'new' types of trained labour and new courses: in business and management studies, technician education, secretarial, social work, nursing, GCE studies and so forth. Thus, as a result of entrepreneurial expansion, many colleges became less tied to the fortunes of local manufacturing industry, particularly in the South-east, and could recruit from a wider intake of full and part-time students than hitherto. Yet, despite the progressive appearance of F.E. at this time, and claims that it offered a genuine 'second chance' of social mobility for working-class youth (Cantor and Roberts, 1974; Bristow, 1976) the vast majority of school-leavers remained outside F.E. and training. According to Hordley and Lee (1970) the main beneficiaries of F.E. at this time were the middle class, who were more likely to adopt F.E. as a 'second chance' or, perhaps more appropriately, a 'second choice' route into employment or higher education (Raffe, 1979).

Thus from arguments so far it would seem that the forces that impelled expansion of F.E. in the 1960s and 1970s correspond more closely to shifts in the occupational structure than to any clearly thought out policy of F.E. and training. Consequently, it is not difficult to discern the motives underlying the diversification of F.E. at this time, which led to the shelving of many low status courses and the upgrading of others. Neither is it surprising that regional and other labour market conditions acted to heighten competition between the colleges, resulting in the proliferation of new courses, which ironically rendered the F.E. system less open and less comprehensive than it might at first appear.[3] It was not until the late 1970s and the early 1980s with the establishment of YOP, and later YTS, that F.E. was able to tap the unemployed and unemployable market made available to it via MSC funds (Gleeson and Mardle, 1980). As on previous occasions the stimulus to broaden the F.E. training base arose in relation to dramatic changes in the youth labour market: in this case its almost total collapse. It is this space that the Department of Employment and its major agent the MSC have sought to exploit in the past decade and that has, somewhat paradoxically, opened up new avenues of training reform.

Since before Crowther, the overall failure to establish a coherent policy for 16–19s has enabled the MSC to make political capital out of existing inadequacies of provision, while at the same time manipulating the entrepreneurial legacy of F.E. to its own advantage. Not only has this secured the government's management of school-to-work transition as a permanent feature of social policy, it has also redefined the relationship between F.E. and the labour market it once served. If such state intervention has enhanced the corporate image of F.E. by redefining its curriculum towards national rather than local objectives (Moos, 1984), it has also drawn attention to the failure of the DES, LEAs and colleges to provide post-school F.E. and training to the majority of school leavers. Although in its earliest days the Conservative government was suspicious, even hostile, towards an expensive quango such as the MSC, it has since recognized the MSC's ideological and tactical significance.[4] Thus, under the aegis of enlightened reform, following on the Great Education Debate (1976–79), the Conservative government, via the MSC and more recently NCVQ, has established direct control over non-advanced F.E. and training and achieved a tighter grip over both the transition and transmission points between school and work. By this method central government has gained direct access to the education system and its resources, and encroached on decision-making territory previously occupied by the DES, LEAs and Unions. This is epitomized in the switch in resources from the rate support grant to the MSC, in order to fund the takeover of 15–25% of non-advanced F.E. work. Clearly such practice represents a distinct break with established social democratic thinking that, until the late 1970s, characterized policy and decision making processes in education.

In rather more positive ways, however, there are those who view what the MSC has achieved via centralized means as both progressive and long overdue. Like it or not, some commentators argue that YTS represents the first major step in providing a coherent training provision for the majority of working class youth (Benson and Lansley, 1987). Elsewhere, YTS has been defended 'warts and all' (Hayes, 1983) as 'a step in the right direction that must be protected against articulate opposition' (*TES*, 20.5.83) – a view endorsed by Watts (1983), who has argued '. . . schools must not permit their confusions and misgivings to hide from young people the fact that

YTS will offer the best way forward available to them' (*TES*, 13.5.83). Briefly summarized, defenders of YTS accentuate a number of positive factors which they see as often overlooked by critics of the scheme:

- YTS offers training for all. It encompasses the vast majority of leavers traditionally denied access to F.E. and training.
- YTS represents a much needed bridge between school and work.
- YTS, in contrast with the traditional apprenticeship, caters for the vocational needs and interests of a wide cross section of young people.
- YTS provides support to school leavers in the transition between school and work, when previously no such support existed.
- YTS represents recognition of the State's responsibility toward school leavers in the labour market, when previously no such recognition existed.
- YTS (and previously YOP) draws attention to the exploitation of young school leavers in dead end jobs, and represents a paid alternative.
- YTS seeks to provide broadly-based training (generic and foundation), premised upon clear curricular objectives relating to skills, competencies and work experience.
- YTS pioneers 'person oriented' curricular approaches, e.g. profiling, guidance and counselling, survival skills, personal skills and so forth, which relate to the trainee's needs and interests.
- YTS seeks a radical reappraisal of the traditional links between school, college and work place.
- YTS represents the first concerted attempt to alter the traditional academic base of the school/F.E. curriculum.

Although the discussion which surrounds such criteria is inevitably more detailed and controversial than appears here, it nevertheless illustrates something of the positive gains seen to have been made via the introduction of YTS. However, if such description accentuates the positive side of YTS it also reflects a rather uncritical and idealistic interpretation of YTS achievements. What remains less clear is what trainees themselves make of YTS. This would seem important given that for a majority of school leavers YTS represents *the* main option into vocational training and employment at the present time. Predictably, perhaps, the evidence regarding what trainees think of their experience of YTS is as varied and diverse as the scheme itself. Understandably, those young people who gain a YTS place linked directly with skilled work and prospects of further education, training and career progression are more positive in their attitudes towards YTS than those whose experiences are more precarious (Clough *et al.* 1987). In Raffe and Smith's (1986) study of a cohort of YTS trainees, 78% felt the scheme was a source of cheap labour, and 72% felt that the scheme was simply a means of keeping unemployment figures down. Elsewhere, evidence drawn from other research studies of YTS students' attitudes repeat an all too familiar message; YTS constitutes a form of 'cheap' or 'slave' labour (Roberts and Kirby, 1985; Horton, 1985; Jenkins and Hutson, 1986). Overall, the evidence indicates a trend for young people to be less favourably disposed to YTS in areas of high unemployment, reflecting an obvious point that an employment-led training scheme serves little purpose if there are no jobs to train for. However, as the following comments from a YTS student indicate, the issue is not simply about work but *suitable* work commensurate with one's training:

> When I left school I was lucky enough to have a place in the Youth Training scheme as a trainee at the local Information Technology Centre and found this a very enjoyable and worthwhile scheme, although I wasn't able to complete it, being lucky enough to find a job (full-time). Unfortunately this job is not the kind of work I would like to have a career in so I am now looking for further employment elsewhere.
>
> (Quoted in Raffe and Smith, 1986)

The telling point here is that the student 'wasn't able' to complete the scheme because a job became available – in this case a job that proved unsuitable (Raffe and Smith, 1986). While evidence indicates that YTS leads some young people into full-time employment, the majority of YTS trainees are being trained either for skills which are not in short supply, or which bear little relation to the eventual jobs obtained. Equally controversial is the move by government to ensure that those under 18, who are unemployed but refuse to undertake training, should not be eligible for social security benefit. According to Lewis (1987) this form of compulsion will have a major effect on young people and further education itself. Each year an estimated 20–30,000 young people do not join YTS, with another 15–20% of the 373,000 who do leaving early to go back on the dole. In these circumstances compulsion will swell YTS by over 50,000 young people, but with little or no account taken of the funding implications involved, or how colleges and employers will respond. If one effect of compulsory training is that employers will withdraw from the scheme, another is that it will prevent young people from enrolling at college to undertake courses of their own choosing. In Lewis's view, at least under the 12-hour and 21-hour rule unemployed students have, in the past, been able to participate in further education without losing benefit, often enrolling on technical, academic or professional courses which are more likely than YTS to enhance their future long-term job prospects.[5]

By removing such choice via changes in Social Security Legislation (Training for Employment, 1988), the government has decided to close a major loophole which threatens its Employment Training Programme (ET) for the long-term jobless. Under the government 'ET' policy (1988) the controversial Job Training Scheme for 18–25 year olds, in which young people essentially work for their dole, is to be scrapped and replaced by a package combining key elements of the Community Programme, and Wider Opportunities Programme, and JTS. Under the new Employment Training arrangements it is now apparent that YTS training for 16–18 year olds should fall in line, ensuring a clear line of progression across the 16–25 age range. In principle the new strategy, designed to give over 600,000 long-term unemployed adults training and employment skills (at a cost of £1.4b) would seem to have much going for it, not least in picking up those who opted out of YTS training or failed to obtain employment when they left the scheme. First, it replaces a disparate array of employment programmes and measures within a coherent package. Second, it apparently reduces conflict with the unions by avoiding the wrangles associated with the JTS and cheap labour. However, by making savings from the Community Programme to fund the new scheme, the principle of paying the 'rate for the job' has been abandoned; and what is really controversial about the new scheme is the decision to pay additional premiums on top of social security benefits on a sliding scale depending on age and marital circumstance. Again, this not only brings into question what is meant by *training* in these circumstances, it also extends the pattern by which the unemployed now work for their benefits.[6] A feature of the new scheme is the introduction of training agents who will act as assessors for the long-term unemployed, interviewing them and then following their progress on the twelve-month programme (Felton, 1987). Thus, if such a scheme would seem to avoid the worst pitfalls of the 'no training, no dole' scenario, it does so in name only. Availability for training has, in many respects, now replaced availability for work in the eyes of the social security system – with the carrot of additional 'premiums' on top of benefit for those who undertake training. In this context, training has little to do with the acquisition of job skills; instead it represents a mechanism for keeping the unemployed on their toes and in touch with a work ethic which has no tangible relevance to them.

Clearly, though such manipulation of training policy and social security arrangements may remove sizeable numbers of 18–25 year olds from the unemployment register, it is questionable how far such compulsory training will produce the 'better educated, better qualified and more flexible labour force' envisaged in the New Training Initiative (1981). The likelihood is, of course, that participation rates in post compulsory F.E. and training will improve dramatically, but with the question mark remaining about the relevance such training has in meeting national skill shortages. Meanwhile, comparative international studies indicate that inadequate skills among the workforce as a whole are directly responsible for British Industry's failure to compete with European and Japanese firms. Poorly trained and qualified workers are linked here with low productivity, which makes it difficult for British firms to compete on an equal footing with foreign competitors. The story is a familiar and often repeated one: nine out of ten German, French or Japanese workers possess vocational skills and qualifications, whereas in Britain less than 10% of shopfloor workers possess comparable skills. The danger is that under YTS and ET, by the year 1993 Britain will have the most trained, least qualified and most unemployable workforce almost anywhere in the industrialized world. The main reason for this is that YTS and ET are *remedial* programmes, mainly designed for the social rehabilitation of the most deprived sections of the population, with little thought given to the occupational and job-related function of training. Essentially, YTS and ET are *political* strategies which, in contrast to the consensual view of YTS outlined earlier on have little to do with making workers or industry more efficient. A more original view of YTS suggests:

- YTS alters the traditional relationship between school and work, and hands over school leavers to employers for more positive vetting.
- YTS has little more to do with producing a more skilled work force than with *placing* people in the social hierarchy of society.
- YTS levels of skill training fall far below existing apprentice training schemes (work experience has replaced experience of work).
- YTS curricular guidelines are limited in scope and ambition, e.g.: (a) an over-preoccupation with measuring and testing for social competence; (b) an uncritical linking of motivation and maturation with vocational training.
- YTS exaggerates the process of 'life management' in training and presents a passive view of the trainee: i.e. adapting, coping, surviving and manipulating society.
- YTS represents a mechanism for regulating previously unregulated social behaviour of youth.
- YTS has wider political consequences, e.g. generating a vocational public without skills or access to employment.
- YTS as a form of training for unemployment does not facilitate the socialization of youth into society, but out of it.
- YTS represents a political strategy for regulating the aspirations of the unemployed, and for controlling youth as a class.
- YTS confirms the collective fate of the young unemployed: its curricular arrangements are rooted in the personality structure (assumed personal and social inadequacies) of the young unemployed themselves.

(Gleeson, 1984)

From this perspective, YTS is not simply a mechanism of social control or cheap labour, nor is it just a means of technically allocating young people to the job market or dole queue. If, in the recent past, YTS could be viewed as a screening device bolted onto schooling, that situation has now changed. Alongside a wide range of pre-vocational developments, including TVEI, CPVE, B/TEC, NAFE and NCVQ, YTS is now part of mainstream compulsory schooling and has become almost *legit*. Thus, despite the apparent vocational realism employed in YTS and related vocational and pre-vocational courses, no discernible link exists between the content of training provided, and the content of work available. Perhaps, not surprisingly, under present economic conditions, given types of training associated with generic and transferable skills are not noticeably in demand by employers. The paradox of training is that such demand has to be manufactured by the State, in this case by government and MSC, and 'sold' back to industry as a going concern. However, even the attraction of 'free labour' under YTS and ET has not been a major incentive for employers to employ such labour. The problem historically is that British industry has only ever really been interested in training a small fraction of school leavers, choosing to employ a majority in unskilled or semi-skilled work. With rising unemployment, coupled with a low school leaving age, it is perhaps not surprising that government has had little option but to cover the 'gap' via further education and training. In the absence of war and national military service (or a convenient colony to which to export surplus labour) the technical training structure has been utilized as the most flexible mechanism both to regulate and mobilize surplus labour, if only to contain it.

Engendering equal opportunities

If one unintended consequence of government training policy is that it has drawn attention to industry's failings, another is that it has exposed wider inequalities in the links between education, training and work. Almost in anticipation of this, and in recognition of critical reaction to its own schemes, both MSC and DES have sought to legitimate the new vocationalism in terms of *equal opportunities* and longer-term advantages which training brings to those who participate.

In practice, however, the rhetoric does not match the reality. According to Ross (1987), after a decade of equal opportunity legislation the picture has changed little for women. In 1986 31% of women on YTS were training in office skills; 29% in community/health services; 10% in sales and personal services – with only 1% in training for technical and scientific skills, two of the skill areas in short supply. Elsewhere, Cockburn (1987) in *Two Track Training* argues that it is one thing for the MSC to express a commitment to equal opportunities for women, and quite another to deliver equal access and equality of treatment. Evidence regarding the difficulties which lie ahead in negotiations with the MSC on such matters can be summarized in Ross's (1987) apt 'lavatorial' account.

> Asked about steps taken to combat discrimination, one MSC Area Board responded: '(We) insisted that facilities be made available to encourage girls to undertake training, for example portaloos made available for trainees on a horticultural scheme'. So that is it, the problem is reduced to one of bodily functions.
>
> This preoccupation with matters lavatorial is a depressing and tiresome

commonplace. When I was a fledgling YTS worker, I had to take a young woman on an interview to a prospective garage placement. I was treated to the by now familiar list of excuses as to why motor mechanics is an unsuitable job for a woman, including 'the work is too heavy' and 'we only have one lav and it's a bit rough'.

Making equal opportunities an active reality rather than abstract rhetoric is far more complex than simply establishing his and her loos. Rather, what is required is a radical shift in perception, to move away from the traditional concepts of men's work and women's work. I recently interviewed 350 fifth form pupils to find out their attitudes towards work in general and YTS in particular. Many young women said that they would be interested in learning skills such as carpentry, painting and decorating and electronics but had been put off by sometimes unsympathetic careers teachers, usually women.

(Ross, 1987)

A major problem with the 'new' vocationalism is that it has become associated with a form of remedial rather than occupational training, which restricts rather than promotes equal opportunities. This is noticeably the case in relation to YTS and other related low level courses associated with compensatory education (Atkinson and Rees, 1982). In the specific case of female participation in nursing, child care and other gender-specific courses, this assumes an even more questionable dimension; here vocational training represents little more than a reinforcement of gender roles and an apprenticeship in home crafts (Blunden, 1983; Gibb, 1983; Skeggs, 1986). Elsewhere, evidence regarding black youth on YTS courses indicates that they are consistently more likely to be allocated to schemes offering inferior opportunities of subsequent employment (Fenton *et al.*, 1984; Lee and Wrench, 1984). The 'Catch-22' for black youth is that no matter which route they take, and no matter what their level of qualifications in comparison with whites, they suffer disproportionate discrimination in the job market (Brown, 1984). This view would seem to confirm the conclusions of a report, which indicated that:

If you had the misfortune to be born in the 1960s, and are therefore seeking your first job in the early 1980s, it does help enormously to be born the right sex and right colour, and into a family with the right occupational connections.

(Lee and Wrench, 1984)

If MSC and government is seen to have taken the initiative by placing equal opportunities on the agenda, by extending provision to those previously excluded from further education and training, it remains less than clear what benefit they derive from their new found experiences. While patterns of participation in F.E. and training by class, race and gender have radically altered in recent years, evidence suggests that the social position of young people has changed little either at college or work (Gleeson, 1985). Thus, despite the widely held view that F.E. and training offers an 'alternative route' or 'second chance' of mobility to working class youth, the evidence reported here suggests the contrary (Raffe, 1983b, 1987; Gleeson, 1983). With reference to both race and gender Further Education can, of course, provide an avenue of individual expression and mobility for some students, particularly when it is *not* tied to employment. In practice, however, F.E. and training are linked with employment and fluctuations in the labour market. Sammons' (1983) study of ILEA school leavers indicates that social class and participation in vocational courses are strongly related. Moreover, she found that the job ambitions and expectations of school leavers with limited academic achievements were found to be significantly determined by sex stereotyping. The question of how the system of further education and training continues to perpetuate existing differences in job skills has also been analysed by Raffe (1983b). Increasingly, part-time further education has, he maintains, been used not to select and prepare a minority of working class youth for middle class jobs, but to prepare a large proportion of working class *men* for careers within the working class. Similarly, Dex (1983) has examined the extent to which F.E. represents a 'second chance' for ethnic minorities. She found that while more young West Indian men and women enrolled on voluntary further education courses than whites, they encountered significantly more difficulties and disadvantages in completing their studies, and making the transition from college to work. More recently evidence from the West Midlands YTS Research Project (1985) indicates that white youth are seven times as likely as Afro-Caribbean, and three times as likely as Asian youth, to obtain employment on leaving school. A similar pattern was repeated in the now disbanded mode A and mode B distinctions in YTS, in which whites predominated in the employment-related mode A schemes, with disproportionate numbers of Asian and Afro-Caribbean students participating in community- and college-based mode B schemes.

Tripartism in the post-16 context

Close inspection of student participation in various types of course suggests that there is an interplay between those race, class and gender divisions so far described and those found within F.E. and training itself (Bates *et al.*, 1984: Finn, 1987). Perhaps not surprisingly, as various training initiatives such as YTS, CPVE, TVEI, Access and related pre-vocational courses have been bolted onto traditional F.E., the existence of hitherto implicit tripartite divisions has become apparent. Though certainly less select in intake than in the past, F.E. now directs its courses to three broadly defined yet distinct target groups. Elsewhere I have described these as:

> the traditional though now declining male *craft* apprentice intake (now including female craft skills: typing, child care, beauty therapy, hairdressing, cookery and so forth);
>
> the *academic/technical* intake of the late 1960s and 1970s: including business,

management and technician studies, secretarial, nursing and social work studies, GCSE and 'A' level studies etc.;

the *tertiary modern intake*: the unemployed and unemployable of the 1980s; the curriculum of which is largely given over to generic skills training, work experience and 'life skills' training.

(Gleeson, 1980; 1983; 1986)

Though in practice far less discrete, such broad divisions indicate something of the patchwork nature of F.E. and training provision at the present time. Hence, tripartism, crude device as it may appear here, broadly reflects and delineates various changes in the youth labour market and the kind of opportunities (or not as the case may be) open to young people. Noticeably the forms of curricular knowledge associated with the different routes not only separate off various categories of student, but they also confirm their status in the labour market hierarchy. At the level of teaching, administrative and curricular relations, for example, these distinctions are made manifest in a number of covert ways. Assessment of the academic/technical students' higher calibre is reflected both in the ways teachers perceive the commitment and motivation of such students (Gleeson, 1980; Avis, 1981) and in terms of the physical resources allocated to them. As the so-called high status element of the curriculum has grown, a tendency now exists to categorize increasing numbers of F.E. conscripts as 'less able', and the courses they undertake as 'Mickey Mouse'.

Much of the teaching and learning, particularly in YTS, takes place outside F.E. – being sited at places of work. In this respect, the tertiary modern sector has a number of distinctive features which separate off this area from the other two. With particular reference to YTS, for example, job opportunities are restricted in the main to unskilled and semi-skilled occupations, previously occupied by unqualified early leavers. Moreover, training tends to be employer led and reflects a low commitment to general education. The most notable difference in curriculum terms is the move away from the development of analytical skills to a preference for 'doing' and activity-based learning in relation to, for example, the replacement of general and liberal education by basic skills and personal effectiveness training. The development of 'social and life skills' is an example of where the primary objective is to adapt to given situations, not to analyse or change them. Thus, a young person on YTS, for example, might be encouraged to develop telephone techniques and dress sense as the primary means of improving chances for future employment, rather than to develop a critical appreciation of those economic, political and social reasons which affect his or her position. When overlaid with images of race, class and gender such 'presentation of self' skills becomes more acute. The implication of this for the student is that he or she can gain employment providing that they can overcome their own personal weaknesses. The message it would seem is that the system can provide jobs for those well spoken and well dressed enough to take them. In other respects, too, these aims demand new teaching techniques: for example, intergroup dynamics, personal education, counselling, use of video and visits and so forth. As long ago as 1968 one writer described such 'progressive' innovations for 'less able' students as a 'slogan for crypto elitists' (White, 1968), fundamentally designed to control rather than to liberate young people. It would seem that very little has changed: the YTS trainee has replaced the 'Newsom Child' and it remains legitimate to experiment with progressive techniques for low status students (Young, 1971),

Following on from this, clear institutional divisions can be identified between the three tiers, with YTS courses and other such 'non-examinable' subjects frequently being shunted out to annexes and temporary accommodation away from the main college sites. YTS courses, even the 'off the job' elements, are increasingly being sited at the place of work, companies either relying on 'buying in' teachers from F.E., hiring their own supervisors (usually working for well below Burnham rates of pay and conditions of service) or opting out. This situation is captured in the *TES*'s leader: Grocer Caters for Own Training Needs (*TES*, 11.9.87) referring to a recent HMI report on Sainsbury's training schemes.

> Like the rest of the distribution industry, Sainsbury's makes little use of colleges for skills training. It started to use colleges for its YTS trainees, but found that much of the college provision was irrelevant and failed to motivate trainees, did not integrate education and training elements, and was not consistent across the 13 colleges used.
>
> It now does most of the YTS training itself, but still uses a few colleges where the courses are of high quality. The report suggests that colleges might adopt much of Sainsbury's training style, including the extensive use of audio-visual aids and of manuals to replace note-taking; the emphasis on practical work, discussions, role-play, and tutorials; and the encouragement of students to manage their own learning.
>
> To get firms like Sainsbury's to use them more, concludes the report, colleges need to be more flexible and recognise that the companies often require programmes tailored to their specific needs.
>
> But short of getting the companies to trust them with their training, colleges may still be able to make some money out of them, it suggests – by renting out classrooms for the companies to use during college vacations.

Such commercial realism has, in different ways, had a noticeable effect on making F.E. compete in the market place. Local authorities too must now compete with private employers to become managing agents or, at the very least, include the off-the-job training element in colleges in order to attract MSC funding and commercial/industrial support. All this has happened at a time when government has been operating a rigid budgetary regime implemented via rate capping and other financial cuts to school, college and LEA budgets. In other respects problems for college funding have been compounded by industry's reluctance to continue with traditional apprenticeships (instead opting for the State financed YTS), this having the effect of reducing or even eliminating day release courses in local colleges. Moreover, in 1984 the government's 'Training for Jobs' legislation enabled the MSC to control 15–25% of the budget in Work-Related Non-Advanced Further Education formerly administered by Local Authorities. Democratic control of the budget through local authorities has been replaced by the 'market philosophy' of the non-accountable MSC. In order to receive funding colleges and authorities must now provide the MSC, DES and NCVQ with development plans for approval, and much entrepreneurial activity now surrounds such planning which involves tight cash limits on teachers, students and courses. In the process, it has become convenient for senior management in some F.E. institutions to rigidly demarcate high and low status curriculum and personnel. As a consequence many colleges have separate pre-vocational and YTS departments and sections, often with a pool of staff identified specifically for this low status work; their status is often marginal and their position contractual under the new costing arrangements. In many ways the ambiguity of their status reflects those whom they teach, with its attendant effects on morale and commitment.

Very importantly the teacher's role has also changed in these growth areas. There is a large amount of administrative, planning and pastoral work associated with the new courses. Teachers are obliged to communicate regularly with managing agents, to organize visits to local industry and places of community interest, to counsel students who, in many cases, have severe social and emotional problems, to raise money for residential visits, often spending weeks, and weekends, away from home and college. Teaching in the traditional classroom-based sense of the word often seems remote from the life of the teacher in the 'New F.E.'[7] The teacher is less concerned with subject expertise and becomes more of a technician regulating and managing situations and events. If, at one level, this change reflects a much-needed move towards activity based learning in F.E., at another, it represents a retrograde step which reduces knowledge in the curriculum to a series of atomized tasks to be accomplished with compliant students. In this respect content and analysis in the classroom are largely eschewed. As Green (1986) observes:

> Lecturers on pre-vocational courses can now spend almost as much time on non teaching duties – like counselling, liaising with outside agencies, careers advice and supervising work experience – as in actually preparing and conducting lessons.

Perhaps, not surprisingly, the MSC now see little point in recruiting well qualified and professionally trained teachers. The ease with which the MSC has been able to redefine the teacher's role has resulted in them recruiting *trainers* to perform teachers' work. Moreover, recruiting the unemployed to teach the unemployed constitutes an effective and pernicious mechanism of social control which again generates conflict between teachers and trainers. In other respects too behavioural disruption, an issue not traditionally associated with F.E., has become a noticeable feature of the 'New F.E.'.

> What is clear, however, is that F.E. is now taking *more* out of teachers — more work, more use of their own time – producing more stress. Worse still, the less teachers move with it, the more it threatens. Just as adolescents make role-models of their teachers, so teachers see their students as symbols of a new situation – just as the situation is threatening, volatile, potentially chaotic, this is how the new F.E. students can appear in some giant self-fulfilling prophecy. The potential for disruption becomes much more prevalent in the system.
>
> (Gorringe, 1987)

While it would be misleading to exaggerate the sort of tripartite divisions so far described, there is little doubt that state training policy for the unemployed has simply added another dimension to the existing fragmented pattern of post-school provision. Cuts in education budgets and the sequestration of rate support funds in favour of the MSC have, moreover, increased the pressure to treat the unemployed as a distinct rather than an integrated group within the broader context of F.E. and training. There is at present enormous pressure on the colleges and LEAs to respond to the training requirements laid down by the MSC; many face the prospect that if they are unwilling to 'service' MSC requirements the MSC will simply look elsewhere and utilize the private sector to satisfy its 'off-the-job' requirements. The problem has been affected further by changing regional and demographic factors, which have intensified competition between schools, colleges and MSC for a statistically declining cohort of 16–19 year olds into the 1990's.

Effects of the 'New F.E.' on teachers and students

One consequence of the rise of the 'New F.E.' has been the attempt by government and employers to change the working practices and conditions of F.E. teachers. The arguments to do away with collective agreements have been supported by the Audit Commission's (1985) survey of further education, which investigated the cost-effectiveness of a sample of colleges, concluding that many courses were undersubscribed and not receptive to local employer requirements. Thus, if the Training for Jobs (1984) legislation signalled the government's intention to reduce F.E. autonomy, by removing rate support grant from LEAs and placing it at the disposal of the MSC, the Audit Commission anticipated the Education Act (1988) by redefining the financial, organizational and curricular characteristics of Non-Advanced F.E. (NAFE). A significant feature of the 1988 Education Act is that it separates out Advanced from Non-Advanced courses – broadly those of a standard higher than 'A' levels – defining them as higher education, leaving further education (NAFE) to cover all other provision for those who have left school. Within this definition Clause 81 of the Education Act (1988) reimposes a duty on each LEA to secure the provision of adequate further education to meet the needs of its local catchment. In one respect, this simply restates the vague terms expressed about F.E. in the 1944 Education Act. In another, perhaps more important, way the 1988 Education Act goes further by statutorily requiring LEAs to deliver central government education policy at the local level. It seeks to do this in three interrelated ways:

- by ensuring that not more than 20% of the governing body of a college will represent the LEA, and that half of the members of the governing body will be required to be either representatives of employment or co-optees. It is the statutory duty of the LEA to ensure that the governing composition is so achieved;
- by requiring LEAs to delegate financial and other powers to further education colleges, thereby handing decision making over to an employer-led governing body with limited LEA powers;
- by empowering such governing bodies with the *powers* to select staff for appointment to the employment of the LEA, and to require the LEA to remove from the college staff whom they consider should no longer work there.

In the circumstances, there can be little doubt that the ratchet of central control has tightened at the local level, reducing the autonomy enjoyed by F.E. in previous decades. Ostensibly, what lies behind such policy is an attempt to rationalize the 'new' NAFE by co-ordinating its disparate strands more effectively. In practice the combined effect of Training for Jobs (1984), the Audit Commission Report (1985) and the Education Act (1988) has been to render F.E. more 'school like', ensuring its responsiveness to deliver national policy at the local level. The central thrust has been to dispense with existing conditions of contract and collective agreements, and to ensure the 'flexibility' of teachers in responding to MSC, employer and government requirements. Traditionally, once appointed at a particular grade, the F.E. teacher worked to a nationally agreed number of teaching (class contact) and remitted hours. Under the terms of the new Education Act (1988) such conditions have been suspended in an attempt to make F.E. teachers more responsive to the changing requirements of the 'New F.E.' from the employer's point of view this is an ideal situation since it offers greater flexibility in deploying and redeploying the work force in response to any new initiative the government wishes to introduce. From the teacher's point of view, however, the new conditions of service are as vicarious and stratified as the 'New F.E.' itself – security of tenure being tied to courses and students which may be here today and gone tomorrow (Gleeson and

Hopkins, 1987). Thus, by exposing teachers to the cold wind of market forces, it reduces their professional autonomy and bargaining position over such matters as curricular decision making, INSET, maximum teaching loads and so forth. Already the use made by MSC and colleges of part-time teachers in F.E. is undermining permanence of contract. In this respect, the most 'flexible' teachers in F.E. are part-timers, and it is no accident that F.E. has experienced casualization of labour as a direct result of such MSC control. The use of more and more temporary contracts (renewed on a yearly basis) is, in some areas, becoming the norm and is a direct result of the MSC's refusal to offer permanence of work to teachers in preference to part-time 'trainers' who are more amenable to control.

In recent years NATFHE (the college teachers' union) has been involved in complex discussions with the management side on issues such as averaging (whereby a teacher's class contact would be defined over a year as opposed to a weekly maximum as already exists), remission and a general redefinition of a teacher's duties. These negotiations have been closely related to the development of the 'New F.E.', since they offer management in F.E. a greater degree of flexibility over the deployment of a constantly shifting staff and student population. Again, the buzz word here is *flexibility*, but for whom? In many ways the 1988 Education Act has foreclosed on such negotiations and represents, alongside Training for Jobs (1984), an imposed settlement which places flexibility in the hands of government and MSC. Within these terms, it is evident that LEAs and NATFHE have their work cut out, certainly if they are to avoid overseeing the dismantling of their own conditions of service and tenure.

In effect, the rules of the F.E. game have changed, opening the way for MSC (or Training Agency), government and employers to have a greater say in the financial administration, decision making and hiring and firing procedures of the 'New F.E.' Despite the obvious signs of resistance on the part of NATFHE, LEAs and colleges to such changes there are signs that LEAs and F.E. institutions have already surrendered a sizeable proportion of non-advanced F.E. to the MSC, and that others, stripped of cash, will soon follow. The danger is that, with the most recent legislation, F.E. will simply become the dumping ground for increasing numbers of dissident and disaffected young people. One consequence of this political and administrative separation is that it reinforces arbitrary divisions between education and training, and marginalizes the unemployed as a separate category with their own 'ghettoized' institutions, curriculum and teachers. Already there are signs, as the figures in Table 2 indicate, that some high attainers and those from non-manual backgrounds have already anticipated what is happening. There is a growing trend for such students to stay on in tertiary or sixth form colleges, rather than participate in F.E. which is rapidly becoming associated with YTS, pre-vocational education, re-sits and lower grade training programmes.[8]

How to broaden the base of F.E. in order to make it more attractive to a

Table 2 DES/MSC study of the movements of 16 year olds after compulsory schooling (1986 cohort)

Fifth-year qualification	*Total population %*	*At school after 16 %*	*FE institution %*
Five or more GCE/CSE (with four or more higher grades)	25	63	30
Five or more GCE/CSE (with 1–3 higher grades)	24	23	36
Five or more GCE/CSE (with no higher grades)	22	11	23
1–4 GCE/CSE (with no higher grades)	14	3	9
None	16	1	2
Socio-economic group			
Non manual	29	48	36
Skilled	41	33	39
Semi-skilled	12	8	10
Unskilled	3	2	3
Other	15	10	12

comprehensive range of students is a hotly contested issue, not least because schools, F.E. institutions, sixth form and tertiary colleges are all in competition for a pool of 16–19 year olds which is likely to drop by 15% to 600,000 by 1990. One message coming from the Audit Commission and HMI's (1987) *Sainsbury's Report* would seem to indicate that F.E. should do more to market itself. However, this ignores the basic inequalities which already exist within local labour markets and the ways in which government training policy itself has ghettoized sizeable chunks of NAFE, thereby reinforcing old prejudices about its status *vis-à-vis* other forms of post-16 provisions.[9] In the absence of any comprehensive policy to deal with such a fragmented situation, a two-tier system of provision has arisen almost by default: one half administered and controlled by the DES and to a lesser extent LEAs, incorporating academic and pre-vocational education, and the other, administered and controlled by the Department of Employment and its major agent the Training Commission, incorporating 'on the job' and 'off the job' forms of training.

Effects on teaching relations

In the clamour for relevance in the curriculum following the Great

Education Debate (1976–79), colleges have been forced increasingly to create syllabuses which reflect the alleged needs of industry. So far it has been noted that in the 1960s and early 1970s, F.E. enjoyed a considerable degree of autonomy in its relations with industry, government and examination boards. At the time this relative autonomy was seen as successfully managing the 'fit' between school and work for a minority of youngsters going into work requiring vocational tuition. However, since the rise in youth unemployment the government has attempted to reduce this autonomy in two ways. First, by allowing the Department of Employment control of the Work-Related Non-Advanced F.E. (WRNAFE) budget, many colleges have been forced to subscribe to the training policies of the MSC. Colleges whose traditional supply of apprentices has diminished as a result of industrial recession have, for example, had little other opportunity than to recruit from trainees made available via YTS and related sources. Second, in setting up the National Council for Vocational Qualifications (NCVQ), the government has ensured that the colleges and examining bodies will provide curricula that subscribe to the needs of industry enshrined in the 'Training for Jobs' (1984) legislation.

If, at one level, the NCVQ would seem a timely device for co-ordinating the hotch potch of qualifications and courses offered by the various competing examination boards, at another, its main brief is to tighten the accreditation mechanism in favour of more employer-led courses. Already the signs are that the major boards such as B/TEC are responding to such changes, often surrendering sizeable educational components of their courses to meet the new requirements of work-based accreditation and assessment. The danger is that in the process vocational education and training becomes little more than a narrow form of work training, with little regard paid to the longer term educational needs and requirements of students many of whom require more time to make decisions about their future.

It is perhaps significant that, whilst the Department of Education will have an advisory role in educational matters, the NCVQ is ultimately responsible to the Department of Employment. Government is, therefore, further centralizing the curriculum at both ends – at its creation and evaluation. Furthermore, the NCVQ has refused to include within its remit so-called academic courses, such as GCSE and 'A' levels. Thus, while those qualifications felt to be in the vocational area will be closely scrutinized, those academic qualifications defined as being broadly in the area of *education* will be left largely untouched in comparison, thereby making access to university and higher education even more difficult for students with 'vocational' backgrounds. It would seem that a bargain has been struck: the DES will continue to caretake the liberal humanist tradition and the Department of Employment (MSC) will police the industrial trainer tradition for everyone else. According to the National Union of Students: 'Young people will be divided into sheep and goats between the two systems (vocational/academic), either at 16, or more likely at 14'.

Perhaps not surprisingly, the NCVQ is made up by representatives from industry and commerce, and those groups that have articulated the sharpest criticisms of comprehensive education. There has been no attempt at mobilizing other interest groups, such as teachers, community leaders, educationists or parents, in developing a system which makes *access* to higher education more open and comprehensive. Again, then, the emergence of a differentiated system can be evidenced if we look at the curricular aspects of the 'New F.E.' Some students will continue to receive a curriculum geared to the needs of Higher Education while a vocational system will develop around the needs and interests of employers whose bottom line is *relevance*. Relevance in this sense is restricted to realistic work oriented learning and skills. In this respect the MSC has taken on board ideas that some regard as having a progressive origin, turning them to reactionary ends. There is, for example, negotiation in courses so that students can to some extent determine their own learning agenda; the problem remains, however, that progression into higher status courses and employment is only available for a select few. The principle of negotiation does not, for example, extend to those courses or forms of progression which students define as relevant. Moreover, this progressive methodology has been adopted sometimes at the cost of specific content, such as the ban on political education and Clause 28, and has failed to challenge notions of sexism and racism that are apparent both at work and in the classroom. Instead, key elements of the 'new' vocational curriculum, for example, emphasize a person-oriented approach wherein skills for living, defined as coping with misfortune, surviving, establishing relationships, handling interviews and so forth, have become the order of the day. The problem here is that in redefining knowledge of the world into a set of skills or tasks, it arbitrarily separates off training from mainstream education and presents society as something that can be transformed only by personal manipulation. One consequence of replacing a knowledge-based approach with a skills-based approach is that it reduces teaching, learning and assessment to a disconnected series of modular tasks which has no overall coherence or logic. In other words, it contains no commitment to general education or to young people learning *about* the society in which they live. As Green (1986) has commented:

> The danger of 'instance relevance' is that in its earnest desire to 'meet the kids where they are at', it ends up leaving them exactly there – in the case of working class kids, in working class jobs, excluded from the culture of power . . . Education without concepts and analytical tools is education for subordination.

Whatever the assumed failings of liberal humanist education to mobilize working class interest and enthusiasm, it nevertheless remains the dominant code through which cultural achievement and power are realized. The dismantling of liberal humanist education for working class students on grounds of 'relevance' is recognition of this. By dismantling comprehensive education development successive government policies (1976–1988) have been able to initiate experimental schemes with low status students on the basis that education is not 'working'. Yet there exists no evidence that the skills so far described represent a genuine alternative for the vast majority of school leavers. Despite the popularly held view that the educational system is preoccupied with academic values there is little to indicate that the criteria governing the new vocationalism either challenge such entrenched values or seek to integrate technical, vocational and academic skills in the curriculum. Moreover, recent evidence suggests that training policy has done little to facilitate a more unified system of post-school provision, or to broaden the patterns of participation in non-advanced F.E. and training (DES, 1985). All the signs are that the policies outlined in 'Working Together' (1986) will reinforce existing divisions and co-ordinate more effectively, particularly with the setting up of the NCVQ, the development of a more pronounced stream in the 16–19 age range. In other respects too it must be recognized that managers in F.E. have generally made far fewer resources available for students on pre-vocational courses than for those on more academic courses. Examples abound throughout the country of pre-vocational students being shunted out to annexes and temporary accommodation away from main college sites. Many F.E. managers have regarded these as low status courses for 'drop outs and dead legs'. Indeed, MSC money, given specifically to help finance particular courses, has been used by some colleges suffering cuts in their budget from the LEA, to finance other areas of college expenditure. Elsewhere, colleges have been seen to plead with local industries for donations of machinery no longer useful to local companies so that students on YTS can apparently develop new 'skills' – so much for the brave new world of tomorrow's technology (Gleeson and Hopkins, 1987).

At the heart of this is the way YTS and pre-vocational courses lack status *vis-à-vis* academic, professional and other job-related programmes, which is acutely reflected in the learning environment, and pay and conditions of both teachers and students. It is, of course, well known that the traditional grading of work in F.E. has in part led to differences in pay, perceptions and conditions of those teachers in so-called academic work from those in allegedly non-academic work (Gleeson and Mardle, 1980). However, the emergence of the 'New F.E.' has helped exaggerate these differences among teachers and students. Although some bodies such as the FEU welcome the introduction of 'activity based learning' and other developments associated with the 'New F.E.', among teachers the view appears to prevail that to teach in this area of 'low level work' is less demanding, and less career enhancing than the more prestigious GCSE and B/TEC First and National work. It is perhaps no accident that most part-timers (the majority being women) teach in this area, without status and possessing inferior chances of career development. One teacher in exasperation put it this way:

> Without deprecating the efforts and achievements of our mainstream F.E. colleagues, it is true to say that our work has many important differences. For example, that staple of regular teaching, the classroom lecture is, more or less, a non starter . . ..
>
> Moreover, there is the demand for continuous assessment usually in the form of time consuming profiles. Similarly, regular, often lengthy meetings with outside agencies, along with routine team meetings, bite deeply into lecturers' time and make further claims on their energies.
>
> One of the biggest differences and perhaps the real motivation behind this letter, is that YTS lecturers are seldom established on a permanent basis and, therefore, are financially and politically vulnerable. Not only are there limited promotion prospects, but there is an all pervasive atmosphere of uncertainty which militates against professionalism . . ..
>
> Despite emphasising the considerable differences that exist between mainstream F.E. and YTS work, it is imperative for us to work together, especially within the framework of our Association. So this is a plea on behalf of YTS lecturers to our mainstream counterparts: take us seriously and pay attention to our needs, interests and concerns at Branch meetings.
>
> (Adapted from: 'Members in YTS: A Plea'. *NATFHE Journal*, December 1984)

In various ways this letter confirms the divisions which many lecturers see emerging in F.E. at the present time. It not only identifies differences in status, but also differences in teaching relations, curriculum and career opportunities. The author's reference to 'mainstream' colleagues – implying that there are those who are *not* regarded as mainstream – indicates something of the widening divisions that have emerged in contemporary F.E. While such inequality of status between different areas of work is not new to F.E., what is new is the way in which government policy reinforces these differences and is now part of the cause. From this viewpoint official exhortations from MSC and government about improving levels of student participation or equal opportunities in F.E. shoud be viewed with some scepticism. The reality at the present time is that vocational education and training provision for the majority of school leavers remains patchy and meets the needs of neither individual or society. In recession, government and employers have abandoned any long-term education and training plans. The folly of allowing employers to dictate training policy will undoubtedly have far-reaching effects, not least in reducing skill levels throughout the workforce. Ultimately, responsibility for this rests with government and the MSC who have failed to establish a coherent *policy* of education, training and work, and who have sought to regulate rather than mobilize the labour force via training. In this respect, the MSC has done little to extend or to improve the quality of further education and training, and has reinforced existing inequalities in provision. The irony is that the MSC has been allocated massive funds to continue in its present role, the long-term consequences of which will be disastrous for standards in post-16 vocational education and adult training. While such funds may keep the colleges and the factory training departments open, there remains ambiguity and doubt about what 'streamed' teachers and students gain from their experience of the New F.E. It is to some of the curricular implications of such streaming that the chapter which follows now turns, with particular reference to the part played by *social and life skills* in the curriculum.

Notes

1. The term 'vocationally uncommitted' is used to describe students staying on at college, but who have not made a decision about their future career pattern.
2. See Notes section in chapter 1.
3. I am grateful to George Mardle with whom some of the analysis presented here was first developed. See Gleeson, D. and Mardle, G. (1980).
4. Although recently MSC has experienced cuts to its budgets it remains a major government spender.
5. Young people have, until recently, been able to study for up to 12 hours without losing benefit, rising to 21 hours after 3 months; this is sometimes referred to as the '21-hour rule'.
6. A feature of changes in social security legislation announced in 1988 under the Conservative government's Employment Training Programme.
7. I am grateful to Mike Hopkins with whom I have worked closely on this and related issues raised in this chapter. See Gleeson, D. and Hopkins, M. (1987).
8. Figures adapted from Ian Nash's article: 'No Place to Hide', *Times Educational Supplement*, 13.11.87
9. See HMI's (1987) report on NAFE: *NAFE in Practice: An HMI Survey*. London, HMSO.

Life Skills Training and the Politics of Personal Effectiveness

3

In recent years much has been made by the present government and its supporters of political and sexual bias in the curriculum. History, sociology and even physics teachers have, for example, been attacked for introducing 'leftist' ideas while others have been criticized for actively encouraging homosexual and lesbian attitudes among young people. Yet, despite the moral panic which tabloid revelations have excited about this matter, HMI, The Secretary of State for Education, LEAs and courts have been unable to detect any significant sign of its existence or positive evidence on which to act. Political bias, of course, often exists in places where one chooses to search for it. In this respect, it is perhaps significant that the Conservative government and its supporters have not chosen to look too closely at the ideological content of government education and training policy itself, in particular at those courses which favour popular images of enterprise culture, self-determination and survival training.[1] It is to this neglected aspect of the present debate about 'bias' in the curriculum that this chapter is addressed.

So far in this book I have sought to demonstrate the ways in which government training policy has reinforced rather than challenged various tripartite divisions within further education and training. It has also been argued that the rise of the new vocationalism marks a response to certain political and ideological imperatives and should not be confused with making either young workers more employable or industry more efficient. Viewed critically, the vocational realism currently associated with the new training paradigm conceals its inherent irrationality; its purpose being to create a vocational public whose eventual employment (or unemployment) bears little relation to the content of their training. Irrespective of the apparent realism employed within recent training initiatives, often associated with jargonized terms such as 'occupational training families'

(OTFs), 'generic skills', 'modular training', 'transferable skills' and so forth, many of the skills involved are of a social rather than a technical or occupational nature.

Nowhere is this better exemplified than in social and life skills training (or, in other guises, 'communication' skills), an area of the curriculum ostensibly designed to complement the cognitive dimension of training. In recent years social and life skills curriculum has emerged to occupy an important place in new training initiatives, particularly those associated with YTS and pre-vocational courses such as TVEI, CPVE, LAPP, RSA, City and Guilds and B/TEC. At one level the attraction of 'life skills' training is that it is relevant and addresses, in ways that traditional Liberal and General Studies could not, the practical problems likely to affect young people in hard times as adults, as parents and as employees. At another, ambiguity surrounds the criteria upon which such social skills for living are constructed and appraised, not least because of their close behavioural connection with altering young people's attitudes toward authority, industry and society. In this respect the more centralized control of this affective domain has made it increasingly difficult to differentiate between the 'official' and the 'hidden' curriculum, not least because the two have become overlain in many ways. With reference to the behavioural objectives associated with life skills training, it is argued here that the hidden curriculum has now surfaced as *the* official curriculum. Here I am referring to the ways in which the implicit ordering of knowledge (attitudes, deference and demeanour, presentation of self and so forth), traditionally separated off from the formal content of the curriculum, has become written down as valid knowledge warranting transmission and evaluation. Perhaps, not surprisingly, in a short space of time life skills training has become detached from the wider objectives associated with social and political education: the point here is that teaching young people *about* society has been replaced by criteria designed to alter their *relationship* with it – a political issue that has hitherto remained ignored.

If this image of vocational relevance has filled a void left by the apparent failure of liberal humanistic education (to provide a more realistic) understanding of society's industrial and commercial values), it has also drawn closer attention to the ways in which radical Conservative political and economic thinking finds its expression in the curriculum. From this viewpoint government training policy does not simply represent a reaction or response to youth unemployment but is also part and parcel of a planned attempt to alter the content of the curriculum in favour of employer-led definitions of reality. In this respect training for 'personal effectiveness' is seen here to have a closer relationship with Conservative government thinking than might first appear; it also represents an important ideological mechanism through which labour is made ready and available for work. Thus, a central feature of 'life skills' is that, in contrast with conventional social and general studies in the curriculum, it is not designed to provide a balanced understanding of society, but to train young people in relevant social skills associated with surviving, communicating, getting on with people, listening, talking and so forth. If, on the surface, such skills would appear relevant and non-controversial, two interrelated factors should be considered. First, 'life skills training' is essentially remedial in orientation and second, the MSC operates an effective ban on political education in such courses.

Thus in view of the recent opinions expressed by the right wing Hillgate Group about the dangers of bias and indoctrination elsewhere in mainstream education, this controversial aspect of government intervention in vocational training has escaped critical attention (Scruton, *et al.*, 1985). If, as Marsland (1987) in his critique of left wing bias in sociology has recently pointed out, '. . . criticism should not be so one-sidedly selected . . .', there is little evidence that the new right has heeded such advice in its selection of what counts as bias in the curriculum.[2] It is perhaps for this reason that this chapter seeks to examine the level of politically inspired thinking which lies behind life skills training and the criteria thought necessary to enhance the 'personal effectiveness' of young people. This would seem all the more important in view of the government's contention that technical and vocational education (14–18) now constitutes a viable alternative for 'that 40%' who fail to succeed in mainstream education (DOE, 1981, 1984; MSC, 1981, 1982a).

Skills training and the presentation of self

Despite the expressed intention of both government and MSC to extend the quality and quantity of training for *all* young people (MSC, 1982b), there is little doubt that the Youth Training Scheme (YTS) is principally directed towards the 40% of school leavers who leave school with only the minimal level of formal qualification (Ainley, 1985). Effectively, YTS and related pre-vocational schemes are designed to remove large sections of 16 and 17-year-olds from the labour market, thereby reducing the statistical level of unemployment. The White Paper (1981) which precipitated the establishment of YTS confidently predicted that its proposals for youth training would enable trade unions, employers, educationists and government '. . . to more clearly see what they need to do for the system to work'. Elsewhere other observers have noted that the White Paper's recommendations marked a significant break between the 'old' (voluntaristic) and the 'new' (corporate managed) F.E. + training system, thereby constituting '. . . the most far reaching proposals for industrial training ever put before Parliament' (*Guardian*, 16.12.81). Essentially, the proposals of the Youth Task Group Report (MSC, 1982a) confirmed and extended the kind of training schemes already initiated by the MSC under the Labour government, but on a larger and more systematic scale.

Yet, in view of recent attempts to create a permanent bridge between school and work, and the policy to extend YTS to two years, proposals for improving the quality of training provision remain limited in scope and design. Already the indications are that the levels of vocational training experienced by YTS trainees fall significantly below those associated with conventional training arrangements and that, under YTS, an eighteen-year-old has less actual work experience than apprentices or other young people working in a full or part-time capacity (Ryan, 1984). What remains less than clear is how 'skills training', '. . . involving basic literacy and numeracy, practical competence in the use of tools, machinery and office operations' (DOE, 1981) will enable young people' . . . to make their way in the increasingly competitive world of the 1980s' (MSC, 1982a). Part of the problem can be explained in terms of the MSC's insistence on creating a range of 'new' experimental 'skills' designed to replace the apprenticeship system and its links with apparently outmoded work practices. As Cockburn (1987) has pointed out, the content of YTS has been developed on guidelines from the Institute of Manpower Studies, whose vocational orientation was favoured by MSC over the more liberal educational principles being pressed by the Further Education Unit (FEU) of the Department of Education and Science (Seale, 1984). Suspicious that educationists might subvert the content of the new vocationalism, MSC preferred the services of occupational psychologists working in areas of skills acquisition. According to Cockburn (1987), in practice the content of YTS training is neither educational nor vocational so much as empty of meaning.

> The Institute's 'transferable skills' (Hayes, 1983) are so basic as to lend themselves to parody: learning to push, learning to pull. Learning to stand up without falling over? Life and social skills, intended by the MSC to be a core element of all YTS schemes, are widely regarded as a patronising slur on young people's personal qualities. Under this theme they are invited to improve their appearance, their interview technique and their approach to authority.

Much depends, of course, on the view one takes of MSC endeavours to shift the emphasis away from subject-based teaching in favour of occupational training which is not specific to one particular occupation. There are those who believe, for example, that the 'skills' approach represents little more than an attempt to run down traditional craft principles in line with government policy on apprenticeship and union control (Moos, 1983; Ryan, 1984; Fairley and Grahl, 1983). Others argue that the curricular guidelines associated with YTS offer a more flexible approach to training than traditional forms allow, and prepare young people in a wide range of generic work skills (Hayes, 1983). At present it is this latter view which enjoys strong official support, and is premised on the assumption that conventional curriculum arrangements have failed the majority of school leavers (Callaghan, 1976). However, it is one thing to draw attention to the inadequacies of the conventional academic curriculum, and the apparent 'failure' generated by it, and quite another to legitimate the new vocationalism in terms of that failure (Hargreaves 1982). Since the Great Education Debate (1976–79) the eagerness with which both the left and right have attacked the apparent inadequacies of progressive and liberal humanistic education has, somewhat ironically, created the space in which the 'skills' based approach has been allowed to flourish.[3]

Yet, to date, government and MSC have offered no tangible evidence that skills training is what industry needs or requires. Since Jim Callaghan's controversial Ruskin Speech (1976) employers have had little to say about the direction which the new training initiatives should follow. They, perhaps more so than government, recognize that the present range of jobs available in the economy are generally routine and undemanding and that, both now and in the future, these jobs will not require a sophisticated level of further education or training (Lee, 1983). Consequently it might be argued that in its present form, the debate about training is meaningless since it is not connected with work (Gleeson, 1983), it simply obscures the real issue of unemployment and the way in which training itself has become a substitute for employment. Thus, despite the government's professed intention of more closely integrating education and work, the indications are that the gap between the two is widening, both as a direct result of training policy and the unwillingness of employers to recruit workers from experimental training schemes.

The problem with this type of critique is, however, that it rather naively equates the success or failure of YTS, and other such schemes, with whether or not young people obtain jobs. While it may not be unreasonable to expect that training should be connected with work, there is no evidence that Government Training Policy is designed to make workers either more productive or employable. One alternative suggestion put forward (Moos, 1983) is that training policy is more administratively involved with establishing new criteria for allocating 17 to 18 year olds to declining job market, at a time when conventional social controls have largely broken down (Bates *et al.*, 1984; Finn, 1987). The problem, if one can refer to it as such, is the excess supply of young adult labour, and the kind of moral panic (or 'structural legitimacy problem', Offe 1967) this presents – real or imagined – to the wider society. However, the part played by YTS, and schemes like it in the process, is not solely one of allocating young people to the job market; it does more than that. The weakness with the job allocation model according to Thurow (1975) and Collins (1979) is that it is too static: it ignores the ways in which emerging formal patterns of vocational education and training actually embody theories of socialization, images of power, concepts of business and so forth which, themselves, become institutionalized as rules at the collective level (Meyer, 1977). From this viewpoint, the structure of training cannot be viewed as separate from the kind of economic and political philosophy which gave rise to it, since they are one and the same thing. An example of this may be cited in the following MSC document, which equates the imperatives of training with the imperatives of national economic recovery:

> As a country, we must set ourselves the aim of achieving urgent and radical changes to our training arrangements. If our industry and our commerce and our work force – both young and adult – are to be adequately equipped to face the future . . . the compelling need, therefore, is for a training system which enables all workers to acquire a basic range of skills and to develop and adapt them throughout their working lives.
>
> (DOE, 1981)

If such remarks contain a familiar message about the co-existence of labour and capital, they also express a consensual view regarding participation in a common class, culture and citizenry. Yet, in terms of training practice under YTS and conventional F.E. arrangements, evidence clearly indicates marked differences in the take up of training and employment opportunities by class, race and gender (Gleeson, 1983; Lee and Wrench, 1984 and Cockburn, 1987).

As so-called higher status technical and academic courses in further education and training have grown, a tendency now exists to categorize increasing numbers of trainees as less able, and the courses they undertake as remedial (Atkinson and Rees, 1982; Blackman, 1987) (see Ch. 2). One consequence of this administrative differentiation of the unemployed from students on other courses is that it reinforces arbitrary divisions between education and training and marginalizes the unemployed as a separate category with their own institutions, curriculum, teachers and so forth. In such circumstances, the young person's ability to find work is thus situated for him or her in vocational training: it represents an objective appraisal, if not confirmation, of the individual's lack of ability and skill to compete successfully in the job market. It is in this way that the collective fate of the young unemployed becomes ideologically represented via the curriculum as a *skills* problem, at the individual level (Atkinson and Rees, 1982; Wellington, 1987). Elsewhere, Lempert (1981) has noted how such organizing principles of vocational training, already an established feature of the educational system in West Germany, reinforce individual differences.

> Corresponding to the profit interests of private firms, vocational education contributes to a very high specialisation (either theoretical or abstract), an abstract achievement orientation (instead of interest in concrete work tasks), hierarchial conformity, low sense of responsibility for other people and for future generations, selfish competition (at the expense of solidarity and co-operation) and the beliefs of self worth of the 'winners', and a lack of self worth among the 'losers'.

As a consequence, the process by which young people come to interact with and anticipate the new training structures involves them, at least to a degree, in coming to terms with the stigma attached to their own sense of failure. Once established, such structures ensure the kind of framework within which trainees themselves will contribute to the maintenance of reified social relations, through their interaction with curricular arrangements which mirror their alienation (Lenhardt, 1981). This is not to say that trainees and their teachers passively accept such criteria. Increasing evidence, in the form of industrial action in the colleges, including student strikes, high drop-out rates and so forth, indicates strong pockets of resistance to MSC initiatives (Ainley, 1985). However, it is equally the case that a number of additional external factors ensure that autonomy and resistance are checked and contained. Here I am referring to the ways in which:

- non-advanced F.E. and training has become absorbed into National Training Policy and constrained by central government dictat;
- the traditional 'voluntarism' of F.E. and training has been curtailed by MSC intervention, the 1988 Education Act and the expansion of corporate examination structures e.g. NCUQ;
- the separation off of F.E. and training from direct contact with production, whereby training itself becomes a substitute for employment.

For the moment it would seem important to recognize that as recession and unemployment have altered the structural conditions of F.E. and training, there has been a need to construct different curricular criteria in order to encourage 'new' forms of social integration and vocational commitment among the young (Durkheim, 1977). According to Offe (1967), training for 'personal effectiveness' represents part of the search for substitute criteria, wherein such characteristics as 'flexibility', 'loyalty', 'involvement' and so forth, are prized more highly than the acquisition of technical 'know how'. There can be little doubt that it is within this prevailing climate that 'life skills' curriculum now flourishes, and is closely associated with the perceived inadequacies of 'less able' unemployed youth. The question remains, of course, whether such skills represent an alternative departure in curricular thinking, or a restatement of what has gone on before. It will be argued in the section which follows that life skills training represents something more than socialization alone, and increasingly assumes a dimension of political importance.

Life skills as a form of vocational literacy

So far, it has been argued that the rise of the so-called 'new vocationalism' marks a response to certain ideological imperatives, and should not be confused with making young workers or industry more efficient. It is not just that the rules governing vocational training permit only a limited expression of intelligence and restrict young people's autonomy, they also regulate the kind of behaviour that is expected of them in terms of their social orientation and readiness to work. According to Moore (1983) the sort of vocational realism currently employed in training conceals its inherent irrationality; its purpose is seen as blocking a coherent social and political understanding of the world of work.[4] Evidence from the Scottish Leavers Study of attitudes among YTS trainees demonstrates a high degree of instrumentalism, both to the scheme and to their own personal situation (Raffe and Smith, 1986). How far the strong emphasis upon private enterprise and self help via training has had an effect on trainees' attitudes remains to be seen. As Lee and others (1987) have noted, the role of training and the labour market itself in educating young people into attitudes of calculative individualism has been relatively neglected. What Lee's study did find, however, was that:

> many of our respondents had been inculcated with individualistic values before they joined YTS but that they nevertheless took its moral lessons to heart in appraising their encounter with the scheme.

To date, the curricular implications of this argument have not been taken up. Perhaps, understandably, the dominant emphasis of critiques of youth training remain focused on the macro elements of training, that is, on the ways in which it represents a substitute for employment, a mechanism of cheap labour, a means of regulating youth labour markets and so forth. Yet, despite evidence which indicates that training does generate a pool of low wage earners, it is the ideological arguments in favour of how private enterprise *ought* to function that is important for understanding the essential curricular ingredients of the new vocationalism (Esland and Cathcart, 1984). As Bates *et al*. (1984) and others (Holt, 1987) have recently argued, it is a mistake to view training policy simply as a knee jerk response to youth unemployment. Instead, it should be looked at in relation to the government's overall political and economic strategy designed to alter social relations in the work place and to restructure curricular priorities around a greater appreciation of industrial and entrepreneurial values. In this respect the kinds of argument which favour generic skills training and training for 'personal effectiveness' do not find their expression in the actual realities of work practice. Rather, they exist in idealized conceptions of how industrial relations ought to operate under free market conditions. The ideological significance of skills training is that it projects the learner within this fantasy as a flexible entity, capable of being employed or re-employed in a variety of jobs and settings. Despite the collapse of youth labour markets, it is within this idealization of the links between work and education that contemporary Tory training policy is located: its aim being to reduce worker dependence on outmoded skills (which are seen to be too closely related to union control and restrictive practices) and to ensure the adaptability of the worker in the face of changing market forces.

Consequently, a major selling point of transferable skills training to employers is not the level of technical skill which it is seen to impart, but the type of flexible labour it produces. The fact that non-advanced further education and training has, since the introduction of the government's training policy (DOE, 1981; MSC, 1981) become less directly connected with production, is now overlooked. Irrespective of the rhetoric of vocational realism employed in the new vocationalism, no discernible links exist between the content of training provided and the actual content of work available. This is particularly noticeable with reference to 'self starting' (Hayes, 1983), an element designed to introduce entrepreneurship into the curriculum. 'Starting your own business' and 'preparing for self-employment' may appear radical in the present context of unemployment, but in practice such concepts do not constitute realistic goals for the majority of school leavers. An alternative view of 'self-starting' is that it represents a euphemism about non-work, and pre-sets young people to think of themselves *outside* rather than *within* the mainstream of society.

If the spirit of individualism evident in such idealism bears the imprint of radical Conservative thinking, it should not be confused with attempts to increase the freedom of choice of the individual. Rather, it is the uncertainty which surrounds young people's employment prospects which legitimates the construction of 'skills training' and which allows the State to 'protect' youth from the inimical influence of unemployment. Thus, within the context of 'life skills' training, 'standing on one's own feet' is not concerned with the individual acting on his or her own initiative, or with making choices. As the following curricular guidelines would seem to indicate, the social skills involved are more closely connected with those of coping, surviving and adapting to a given view of the world:

> We would like to see life skills as the all embracing term. Life skills could then be divided into 'Social Skills' and 'Coping' (or Life Management) Skills. 'Social Skills' would include more than face to face contact, since people may relate to others via letters, the telephone, and on a group or individual basis. 'Coping Skills' would include dealing with everyday apparatus and procedures, such as using a public telephone, filling forms, reading maps, finding accommodation and so forth.
>
> (FEU, 1980, *Developing Social and Life Skills*)

There is, of course, little here that is new. Essentially, life management in this context does little more than evoke the traditional and often patronizing rhetoric of liberal and social studies in the 1950s and early 1960s, which emphasized citizenship, form filling, technical report writing and other such skills. Perhaps, not surprisingly, the same criticisms of that approach apply now as they did then (Gleeson and Whitty, 1976). Society as such is not thrown open to question; instead it is the individual who is required to modify his/her behaviour in relation to the 'realities' at hand. Moreover, the publications designed to serve this new market reinforce this person-orientated approach wherein skills for living are defined mainly in terms of coping with misfortune, establishing personal relationships, handling interviews and the ever-present use of the telephone (Pring, 1985b). The danger here is that by redefining knowledge of the world into a set of atomized skills it separates off training from all other forms of knowledge and presents society as something which can be successfully overcome via manipulation.

Within this context 'standing on one's own feet' is not concerned with the individual acting on society, or with young people struggling against the forces that entrap them.[5] Essentially, the life management approach to 'SLS' training emphasizes individual *adaption* and *survival*: society as such is not thrown open to question other than in the narrowest of entrepreneurial terms – 'you can make it if you try'. Thus, despite the apparent veneer of social relevance in SLS there is little reference to the individual learning about society, or of the student acquiring knowledge and concepts which take him/her beyond the immediate and the parochial. When written down there can be little doubt that some of the basic skills young people are expected to learn take on a quite pedestrian appearance (Seale, 1983).

Reading numbers
Counting
Measuring length or distance
Reading words
Listening to get information

(Freshwater, 1982)

Again, the only items missing here would seem to be walking, eating and use of the telephone. However, the brevity of such checklists is by no means isolated. Consider, for example, the MSC's view of the skills which *trainers* are expected to evaluate in young people under the heading, 'The world outside employment' (Table 3).

What is perhaps most 'revealing here is the' preface that describes the checklist as 'a variety of skills and knowledge which when understood can assist a young person to develop within the community as a whole'. Elsewhere in the same notes of guidance, 'personal effectiveness' is measured in terms of the trainees' ability to 'talk to strangers', 'be polite and helpful', 'behave in the right way', and so forth (MSC, 1984). In this respect the curriculum supporting such basic skills represents little more than a crude attempt at colonizing everyday life (Atkinson, 1983), linked with filling in forms, opening accounts and generally 'being good'. Not

Table 3 The world outside employment

	Not Yet	Yes with Help	Yes
The importance of keeping clean			
How to use a bank or building society			
How to plan money			
About any staff discounts, the social club, etc.			
How to be loyal to the work-place			
What people expect of each other away from work			
How to apply for a job			
How to use the telephone			

(MSC 1984)

only does this kind of prescriptive approach fail to get to grips with the very real educational and learning difficulties that affect young people, but it also conveys an implicit assessment of their position and worth in society. One consequence of this is that trainees are made more aware of what mainstream society expects of them, in terms of attitude, behaviour, motivation and so forth, but which as *outsiders* is nevertheless beyond their reach.

Under these circumstances youth training represents little more than a particular form of mass vocational literacy that shifts responsibility for the reproduction of workers back on to themselves. Training the unemployed not only enables them to 'stand on their own two feet' (after all, we trained them) but also seeks to handle the perceived workers' reproduction deficiencies, i.e. their lack of basic skills. By making workers more responsible for their own destinies – epitomized in the terms 'on your bike' (Norman Tebbitt, 1983) and 'taking your skills with you' (Hayes, 1983) – in this way no recriminations can be made against employers or the state, since it is the market that is the deciding factor. In this respect training policy simply replicates nineteenth century liberal economic thinking: the point being to have an unlimited elastic supply of labour the quality of which is not *that* important (Broady, 1981). As the following newspaper advertisement, sandwiched between second-hand cars and situations vacant, indicates, YTS labour can be 'conveniently' marketed and packaged like any other product.

> Work Experience Places Wanted – No Cost to Employers. School-leavers who have been professionally trained in typing and other secretarial subjects by Sight and Sound are available for work experience with Central London employers under the Youth Training Scheme. No cost to employers, no paperwork. Please ring our YTS Liaison Officer for full details.
>
> (*London Evening Standard*, 25 October, 1983)

While there is, of course, no clear evidence that basic skills training has any direct effect on young people's attitudes, it is perhaps what gets left out of the curriculum that is important: notably the absence of any general and political education. Yet recent attempts to keep politics out of training (Morrison, 1983) have ironically only drawn attention to this neglected area. Peter Morrison's now famous proclamation that 'I am totally convinced that the youth training scheme is all about the world of work, and I don't want it to get a bad name if politics got involved' (*The Times Educational Supplement*, 23 September, 1983) has, if anything, increased public suspicion of the MSC's political ambitions in redefining curricular priorities in this area. Despite attempts to play down the censorship of political education in YTS there can be little doubt, as the following communiqué from the MSC to managing agents makes clear, that politics has little to do with learning about British industry:

> Managing agents should note that their agreement with the Commission requires that the training programme be run in a 'manner acceptable to the Commission'. A key requirement will be that it is not involved in any activity of a political nature or any activity likely to bring the Commission into public controversy or discredit. If this requirement is not met it could result in the immediate closure of a programme.
>
> (MSC, 1983)

It would seem from such remarks that the debate about 'teacher accountability' has shifted in a direction unforeseen by the DES in the immediate years following Jim Callaghan's Ruskin College speech (1976). Despite the problem of how to teach trainees about work without reference to the wider structures of society, such directives convey a political message regarding the MSC's view of training, and its own standing with government and employers. Perhaps this explains why the MSC has chosen to opt for 'guidance and counselling' as a more acceptable means of fostering in young people those skills that will enable them to adopt 'the right role at work' (MSC, 1983). Closer inspection of the meaning of this phrase indicates that 'acceptance of authority', 'taking orders' and 'work skills' represent the most significant core elements of the skills involved (MSC, 1977; 1982b). Quoting from MSC guidelines, Seale (1983), for example, detects a 'semi-punitive' approach to counselling:

4.2   The role of the counsellor
He/she must be aware of
4.2.1 any change in work performance against the trainee's norm

4.2.2 signs of alienation in matters of time-keeping, discipline etc., and
4.2.3 any unsatisfactory relationships.
Any of the above must be seen as a need for counselling.

(MSC guidelines quoted in Seale, 1983)

Here counselling is seen by Seale as little more than a mechanism for policing the individual's motivation towards work, and providing essential information for inclusion in his/her personal profile. No less remarkable is the MSC's appraisal of the skills essential to what it terms 'a satisfactory private life' (MSC, 1977; 1982b), wherein the skills of 'making friends', 'resisting provocation' and 'making conversation' represent the extent of MSC thinking on the subject.

That this is all there is to life, or that such limited conceptions eschew political involvement, reflects a particular ideological position presenting training as a neutral mechanism necessitated by individual rather than structural constraints. From this position questions regarding how industry is organized and managed, how wealth is accumulated, how wages, skills and allowances are legitimated and sustained, can be conveniently edited out of training as politically extraneous. The political effect, however, is to separate off the study of work from the society that surrounds it, thereby reducing the entire framework of industrial matters to a narrow set of technical propositions. As a consequence, 'learning about British industry' and 'entering the world of work' become little more than euphemisms for learning about one's place. It is within this overall structure that trainees' political horizons are controlled and their broader vision of the issues and possibilities surrounding them severely restricted.

It has been the argument of this chapter that the call to extend skills training has, in reality, very little to do with changes in production or with the desire, expressed in official jargon, to produce a '. . . better equipped, better educated and better motivated labour force' (Task Group Report: MSC, 1982a). However, it would be misleading to assume that the mismatch between policy objectives and training practice affords teachers and students space in which to renegotiate a more realistic curriculum. As we have seen in the previous chapter non-advanced F.E. and training is at the crossroads between its voluntaristic tradition and the newer compulsory elements that have come to challenge it. Since the emergence of the new vocationalism, the degree of decentralized autonomy in F.E. has been increasingly brought under control by centralized measures designed to incorporate F.E within the wider context of Government Training Policy and the Law. Moreover, recent attempts to reshape college and LEA budgets to make them more receptive to the dictates of the 1988 Education Act and MSC initiatives has ensured the central place of government in structuring national priorities in the sphere of F.E. and training curriculum. In this respect the government and MSC's unprecedented manipulation of both non-advanced F.E. and youth labour markets has elicited strong reaction on the part of teachers and students, involving various types of protest and industrial action. However, the problem that such teachers and students face in opposition to new training measures is that the main political parties and trade unions accept the role of the MSC, or Training Commission, as better than nothing and YTS as a necessary evil. This is perhaps best exemplified in Neil Kinnock's denunciation of a major strike by pupils and trainees over job prospects, in which he condemned participants as a 'bunch of dafties' (Ainley, 1985). However, as I have sought to demonstrate in this chapter, it is not simply economic exploitation that young people face in training but also political exploitation – not least in terms of bias and experimentation associated with 'skills' training.[6]

Whatever the assumed failure of liberal humanist education to 'come up with the goods' (Callaghan, 1976), there exists no evidence that the skills so far described in this chapter represent a genuine *alternative* for the vast majority of school leavers. Despite the views held by successive Education Ministers that the educational system is preoccupied with academic values there is little to indicate that the criteria governing the new vocationalism either challenge such entrenched values or seek to enhance the status of really useful forms of knowledge in the curriculum (Dale, 1986). Indeed, recent evidence indicates that training policy has done little to facilitate a more unified system of post school education, or to broaden the patterns of participation in non-advanced F.E. and training (DES, 1985). But perhaps the main weakness of current training policy is that it is not connected with productive work; it neither identifies appropriate technical skills nor provides an adequate general education for the vast majority of school leavers. From this perspective training takes on a different meaning to that traditionally associated with training for work: here the concept of schooling for the social and political order would seem a more accurate description. It is to this neglected aspect of the present debate about the politics of training that this chapter is addressed – and it is to some of the issues associated with the rise of pre-vocational education that the chapter which follows now turns.

Notes

1. The New Right is highly selective about bias in the curriculum, particularly in relation to social, political and sex education. Positive images of capitalism and profit do not, however, figure in the Right's definitions of 'bias' in the curriculum.
2. Marsland (1987) has criticized sociologists for being biased against business. Yet, in calling for greater objectivity Marsland falls into the same trap which he criticizes others for falling into, namely, that he too is selective and one sided about the apparent virtues of Business and Industry. By aligning himself with the New Right, Marsland confuses sociologists' criticisms of Business and Industry with bias, thereby reducing the significance of his own arguments.

Accusing others of bias has become a convenient way of saying to someone that one does not like what they say. If the central task of sociology is to provide evidence in the support of argument, in order to ensure objectivity, then Marsland certainly does not meet his own criterion.

3. See, for example, Wellington, J. (1987) *Skills for the Future* in Holt, M. (1987) '. . . the language of skills so often used in publications on vocational education is frequently biased towards a behaviourist, psychomotor conception of skill. That conception involves, in a sense, abstracting skills from any particular context or knowledge base. . . .' (p. 39).

4. In this sense 'SLS' should not be viewed as the 'opium of the people'. Perhaps the real issue is what gets left out of SLS curriculum, as much as what is included.

5. I am grateful to Geoff Whitty with whom these and other viewpoints in this chapter have been explored elsewhere. See Gleeson, D. and Whitty, G. (1976).

6. This is particularly pertinent in view of changes in social security legislation (1988) forcing the unemployed into training, in order to secure benefit.

Pre-vocational Education for a Change

4

Following the previous discussion of life skills training, this chapter looks at the broader impact of pre-vocational education within the existing framework of education and training. The term 'pre-vocational education' represents a convenient description which glosses over a wide range of interrelated initiatives, including TVEI, CPVE, and some B/TEC, City and Guilds, RSA and other programmes.[1] Since the introduction of the Conservative government's New Training Initiative (1981) and before, a proliferation of such courses has emerged, including the Low Attaining Pupils Project (LAPP) sponsored by the DES and, more recently, the Joint Board's Foundation Certificate in Pre-vocational Education, designed to rationalize provision at the 14–16 and 16–18 age levels.[2] What these DES and other such funded developments have in common, apart from a close association with MSC initiatives such as YTS and TVEI, is a general integration between the educational and the occupational system, linked with a progressive behavioural approach to skills training 'which constrict, legitimate and enforce new definitions of educational knowledge'. (Moore, 1987).

In a relatively short time pre-vocational courses have radically altered the face of the school and F.E. curriculum, providing a network of courses, qualifications and routes linking school, college and work across the 14–19 age range. Pre-vocational education is not, however, new: it finds its expression in Reports from Hadow to Newsom, in Projects pioneered by Nuffield and the Schools Council, and in craft, design and business courses sponsored through the GCE, CSE, BEC, TEC, CGLI(365), RSA and other such bodies, now often defunct. Throughout the 1960s and 1970s many schools and colleges could, for example, claim expertise in areas associated with business education, craft, industrial studies and work based experience. Perhaps what is 'new' about the new vocationalism of the late 1980s is the centralized degree of expression pre-vocational education now finds across the 14–19 curriculum. In various ways pre-vocational courses overlap and interconnect in a labyrinth of ways. TVEI, for example, in addition to its links with GCSE and YTS, is also accredited by C. and G., B/TEC and RSA qualifications. Similarly CPVE has at one level become integrated with YTS, while at another it complements and connects up with TVEI, B/TEC and other Joint Board initiatives such as the Foundation Certificate in Pre-vocational education and the DES Low Attaining Pupils project (LAPP).[3] According to Stokes (1987):

> The TVEI and CPVE are the most major changes to have taken place in the UK since the number of technical schools, which offered both general education and technical, craft and commercial skill training, began to decline following Circular 10/65. On at least two counts, TVEI and CPVE are important innovations. The first is the firm intention of the government to learn from schemes elsewhere and to support elements linked to economic growth. The other is the uniqueness of TVEI in not only bridging the curriculum divide, but also in spanning the ability range and emphasizing equal recruitment of boys and girls. The CPVE is most significant because it provides a route for those pupils, many of whom underachieve and most of whom are unmotivated, for whom the present curriculum is becoming irrelevant. As such, it will provide a pathway to further vocational training or work.

There can be little doubt that at the present time pre-vocational education is experiencing something of a boom period, enjoying political and media hype as well as attracting categorical funding at a time of cut-back elsewhere in the system. Yet, despite the apparent 'popularity' of pre-vocational courses, their role *vis-à-vis* mainstream education and training remains tenuous and obscure. To many parents, students and teachers pre-vocational education represents a minefield of courses and strange abbreviations which they find bewildering and confusing. In other respects too pre-vocational courses sit uneasily in institutions geared mainly to 'recognized' teaching subjects, methods and qualifications. This situation is compounded by the fact that, in contrast with many other European countries, pre-vocational education in Britain is a relatively recent concept seen by traditionalists as an interloper lacking any clear definition or direction. Thus, despite its broad orientation, backed by contemporary notions of vocational relevance, pre-vocational education occupies an imprecise middle ground between conventional academic and traditional training courses. In various ways pre-vocational education parallels Bernstein's (1971) analysis of the conflict which exists between integrated and specialist educational codes, which betrays wider principles of power and conflict in society. According to Radnor, *et al.* (1986) CPVE, for example, carries a whole set of profound challenges to the three basic systems of the curriculum outlined by Bernstein (1971): content (what counts as valid knowledge), pedagogy (what counts as a valid realization of knowledge) and assessment (what counts as valid evaluation of knowledge.[4]

> Employing Bernstein's analysis, as far as content is concerned, two changes underpinning CPVE are significant. First, there is the role played by vocational studies and work-related knowledge. There is a deliberate attempt to articulate school work with the world of work. The work experience placements also have a role in this. Academic knowledge for its own sake is not encouraged. Thus mathematics is transformed into numeracy, English becomes communication and social studies becomes industrial, environmental and social studies. There is also a shift from the purely cognitive to enactive forms of, or presentations of, knowledge, that is from knowledge to skills (objective and transferable rather than specific task skills: Cohen 1984). Finally, there is an important change in the relationships between knowledge components: a change from strong boundaries between subjects, to weak boundaries, from a collection to an integrated code. The emphasis is upon integration.
>
> (Radnor *et al*. 1986)

Whether or not the integration code associated with CPVE actually challenges the traditional collection code which Bernstein has described elsewhere (Bernstein, 1971) remains to be seen. For the moment, it would seem pertinent to focus on some of the integrating factors which characterize pre-vocational education across the board. Although a number of important differences characterize the range of pre-vocational courses on offer, in terms of their background and ethos many common factors unite them. With reference to B/TEC Foundation Courses, CPVE and TVEI, for example, these common factors include a commitment to:

- cross-curricular and inter-disciplinary enquiry, linking technology, business, design and environment issues, across the ability range;
- a broadening of teaching methods and types of assessment;
- modular and unit approaches to curriculum development, associated with active learning strategies;
- an emphasis on group and project work associated with problem solving and enterprise skills;
- coherent progression and links between school, college and work;
- developing equal opportunities in relation to gender and race.

In many respects pre-vocational courses founded on such progressive principles acknowledge weaknesses in traditional forms of education designed to meet the academic and training needs of only a minority of school leavers. However, pre-vocational education is not primarily an educational concept, it is also an economic one, rooted within the ideological framework of both Labour and Conservative economic thinking. In the Government White Paper *A New Training Initiative: The Need for Action* (1981) investment in training is, for example equated with economic growth: what the White Paper calls for is '. . . a better educated, better trained and more adaptable work force'. Elsewhere, pre-vocational education is seen as part of a wider and continuing policy to bring education and industry into a closer working partnership, to '. . . open to young people within education, across the whole ability range, a technical and vocational route to recognised national qualifications' (Training for Jobs, 1984).

More recently the Prime Minister in her speech to the Conservative Party Conference (1987) argued that industrial competitiveness requires a broader skill base from which to recruit labour and that, to a considerable extent, Britain's international economic decline has much to do with its failure to invest in relevant vocational education and training and, in particular, in the spirit of free enterprise. Seen from this perspective the development of pre-vocational education represents both a challenge and a threat to mainstream liberal education. At one level initiatives such as TVEI, CPVE and B/TEC Foundation and First Courses, have forced schools and colleges to reconceptualize the processes through which they plan whole school development. At another, there is concern that pre-vocational courses, at both the school and college levels, operate independently of rather than integrated within mainstream educational developments. In Pavett's view (1986) support for progressive educational principles associated with pre-vocational courses has blinded many to the socially divisive effects of the new vocationalism, namely, its pre-occupation with what Sir Keith Joseph described as 'that forty percent of disaffected school leavers'. According to Pavett, it is quite consistent to support the educational principles associated with pre-vocational education, but this should not inhibit criticism of ways in which government, MSC and Examination Boards have influenced its direction at local and national level. There can be little doubt that the debate about pre-vocational education has elicited strong emotional reactions among 'believers' and 'dissenters' which, in many ways, has limited the sort of critical discussion which Pavett calls for. It is to this neglected aspect of the present debate that this chapter is addressed.

A basis for choice?

The reasons for the rise in pre-vocational education are complex and, at least in part, find their expression in political and economic circumstances leading up to the so called 'Great Education Debate' (1976–79). There can be little doubt as we have seen that the expansion of vocational training initiatives since that time has much to do with rising levels of unemployment and the collapse of the traditional youth labour market. However, many of the arguments about injecting greater vocational realism into the curriculum, and increasing the participation rates of school leavers in training, go back to the Crowther Report (1959), and beyond that to the 1944 Education Act itself. Somewhat ironically, youth unemployment has drawn attention to the failure of the market mechanism to regulate the effective transition between school and work. Moreover, up to the mid-1970s relatively full employment obscured from view the fact that a significant number of school leavers were leaving school with few if any formal qualifications and entering unskilled or semi-skilled work. Again, if unemployment did little more than cut off the traditional escape route of working class youth into such employment, it also drew wider attention to the exploitation of such young people in the labour market not to mention the nation's internationally poor 'staying on' rates.

Yet, notwithstanding the expansion of comprehensive education in the 1960s and 1970s, the depressing reality is that British industry and commerce has shown very little interest in the broadly educated school leaver. Essentially the skill requirements of the economy have traditionally been met by a narrow apprenticeship system backed up by selective 'in house' training for a small minority of academically or technically able school leavers. This situation is reflected in figures published as late as 1981 by the MSC (1981) revealing that in France 40% of young people entered full-time vocational education after completing schooling, and only 10% in Britain; in Germany 50% entered apprenticeship and only 14% here. Consequently, the percentages from France, West Germany and Britain who started work or became unemployed at that stage were 19, 7 and 44 respectively (Tipton, 1983).[5]

Paradoxically, the rise of youth unemployment has not only initiated long overdue training reforms, it has also revived many of Crowther's original proposals. In various ways YTS, TVEI and related pre-vocational courses incorporate a wide range of progressive teaching approaches initiated in the 1960s and which are, somewhat ironically, now claimed as their own by government and the MSC (see *Better Schools* 1985). Since 1984 emphasis on enrichment of the curriculum, active learning, modular development and assessment linked with problem solving and practical skills, has become noticeable. Moreover, by linking TVEI with the delivery of GCSE and the National Curriculum, and a more effective policing of pre-vocational courses via the National Council for Vocational Qualifications, these objectives have become more commonplace. In both school and F.E. there is now wider recognition of the need to appeal to a broader student audience: already the signs are that YTS, TVEI, CPVE and, more recently, B/TEC, C and G and RSA pre-vocational courses have, in different ways, nudged traditional teachers and institutions into developing learner-oriented approaches which involve cross-curricular developments.

Pre-vocational courses are not, of course, new and have existed in many schools and colleges over a period of time under a number of guises, including 'foundation', 'industrial', 'business and social' studies. The

1970s, however, witnessed a general firming up of the title 'pre-vocational' with the introduction of UVP (1976) (Unified Vocational Preparation Courses), YOP (1979) (Youth Opportunities Programmes) and City and Guilds 365 (1980–81). Alongside such initiatives, however, existed a hotch-potch of vocational courses sponsored by City and Guilds, RSA, BEC and TEC, all in competition for a declining cohort of 16–19 year olds. Following on the Great Education Debate (1976–1979) the Mansell Report *A Basis for Choice* (1979) put forward radical proposals to reform pre-vocational education provision and to rationalize existing bottlenecks in provision. However, the recommendations of the Mansell Report were not taken up until the mid-1980s with the introduction of CPVE, by which time YOP and YTS had already emerged and the marriage between BEC and TEC, to form B/TEC, had taken place. In the circumstances, the attempt to replace B/TEC General, CEE and City and Guilds '365', with a pre-vocational qualification *for all*, failed to materialize, not least because B/TEC anticipated events by circumventing the potential competitive impact of CPVE.

Yet, despite such manoeuvrings it was not until publication of ABC that politicians, educationalists and others took note of the major curricular issues involved in this neglected area of educational debate. In anticipating YTS, CPVE, the Joint Board and much that followed, ABC was well ahead of its time, focusing specifically on the needs of school leavers for whom GCE studies, training or apprenticeship were either unsuitable or unobtainable. Even allowing for changes taking place in comprehensive and further education in the 1960s and early 1970s, retake 'O' levels, or prescribed training courses, were the main career avenues open for the majority of leavers. At the time, as we have seen, access to further education was very much dependent on being *in* employment, or in such high status skilled employment that it warranted employers releasing young workers for further education and training. If, at one level, this situation discriminated against the majority of young people entering unskilled or semi-skilled work, the same was true for returners, many of whom failed their GCE retakes, only to join the ranks of the unemployed one year later. What ABC did was to alert government, teachers and educationists to the predicament of such school leavers. Perhaps, more importantly, it offered an alternative curriculum model designed to meet the needs of the 'average', and increasingly unemployable, school leaver.

The guidelines and advice provided by ABC, although ignored at the time with the hasty post-YOP introduction of YTS, have since informed wider debates about the direction of pre-vocational education. Essentially, ABC has been influential in two ways. First, it sought wider recognition of the vocational and education training requirements of 'that 40%' of school leavers so far referred to, but previously ignored by Government Further Education and employers. Second, it demonstrated that repeat doses of the kind of narrow academic curriculum which had failed young people would be no longer acceptable to them. In so doing, the report offered certain practical curricular guidelines based on a 'core skills' approach specifically designed to meet the needs of the *vocationally uncommitted*. In contrast, therefore, with traditional subject-based approaches, often associated with passive learning and didactic teaching, ABC proposed an integrated, multi-skills alternative approach, linking participatory learning activities with a wide range of core learning and work experiences.

There can be little doubt that the concept of integrated learning has been given further impetus with the introduction of CPVE, B/TEC and the two-year YTS programme. Thus, in many ways, ABC represents an important benchmark, anticipating the need to provide an alternative curriculum to a 'new' and expanding audience. However, if ABC influenced thinking about the new vocationalism, it did not immediately influence policy where it mattered. The initial task facing government in erecting youth training schemes in the period 1979–83, was essentially pragmatic and designed to mop up large surpluses of young unemployed labour. As various critics have noted, the MSC's role during the period was one of crisis management (Dale, 1985) with curricular ideas following on policy decisions already made on the hoof. Recognizing the long-term nature of youth unemployment, however, the Conservative government soon realized the importance of altering mainstream education to accommodate its initiatives. In order to do this, it had to win public acceptance of its policies and, at the same time, change the attitudes of teachers, pupils and parents in schools and colleges in order to make them more receptive to the new vocationalism. Thus, by the mid-1980s Tory thinking about the content of the curriculum gradually caught up with the policies which it had set in motion. Following on the establishment of NCVQ and MSC control of work-related NAFE, the government increased YTS from one year to two, and announced the extension of TVEI beyond its pilot phase. Publication of the two influential White Papers *Training for Jobs* (1984) and *Better Schools* (1985) signalled the government's commitment to extend pre-vocational education to low attaining pupils, and to bring reluctant LEAs and teachers into line via grant related INSET programmes and the Education Act (1988).

Thus, in contrast with previous decades when only a minority of students participated in vocational education and training courses in school and F.E., large numbers in the 14–19 age range now spend increasing periods of time in curricular areas associated with work experience, design, technology, link courses and vocational preparation schemes. Following on recent examination reform associated with NCVQ, SEC and GCSE, the expansion of pre-vocational courses, in particular TVEI, B/TEC, Foundation and First Courses, CPVE and closer liaison between schools, colleges, employers and work via YTS, further education and training has taken on a more comprehensive appearance. The recent piloting of CPVE as an option for YTS 'off the job' training mirrors this progressive view. Part of the explanation of this marriage of convenience arises from the improved image of the two-year YTS, and part from a need to legitimize YTS as both a vocational *education* and a *training* initiative. The philosophy of CPVE, offering as it does a more student-centred and negotiated approach, has been used to enhance the practice and to improve the standing of YTS schemes with parents, schools and colleges. Though to some this heralds a major breakthrough in delivering the illusive vision of F.E. 'for all', to others it is simply a convenient mechanism for dumping 'less able' students in low status streamed courses which lead nowhere. It is to this and related questions about the status of 'pre-voc' alongside others that I now wish to turn.

CPVE and all that

A common feature associated with pre-vocational courses is that they are *progressive*; they explore experimental pedagogies, involve greater student participation and advocate active learning strategies. In various ways the newer courses make greater use of cross-curricular materials, are less subject specific and involve staff working together in an interdisciplinary fashion. TVEI, CPVE, B/TEC, RSA and CGLI have all, in various ways, encouraged the development of modular approaches to curriculum organization and have advanced new assessment techniques, in particular profiling and records of achievement. Moreover, there are increasing signs of cross-referencing between different pre-vocational courses involving accreditation and transferable credits across previously impenetrable department and subject boundaries. Thus, by their very nature, such courses are designed for a wider intake of students than hitherto allowed by academic or trade training courses. This has resulted in the demand that school and F.E. should rethink their organizational and curricular structures to encourage greater movement and progression across the 14–19 age range. A characteristic feature of pre-vocational education is that it should provide young people with a broad range of vocational skills which will enable them to make the most appropriate choice of further education and career development. Nowhere is this better exemplified than in CPVE, a course which aims to provide a core curriculum to enable students to develop a range of competencies across a spectrum of occupations.

CPVE embodies many of the principles enshrined in the ABC report. Essentially it is designed for students who have not yet decided on a particular occupation and who are not going on to take further GCSEs or 'A' levels. A feature in common with other pre-vocational developments is that CPVE provides students with a variety of learning experiences, teaching and assessment strategies. There is an emphasis on learning by doing, group work, independent study, work experience and project work. CPVE offers students five main areas of vocational study to choose from, and, within these areas there are a number of clusters from which they may make further choices. In its rather unfortunately titled document *The Right Pegs in the Right Holes* the Joint Board (1987) outlines the main 'skills' involved, as illustrated in Table 4.

Table 4

Vocational Skills	
Business and Administrative Services	– Organization of Business Services to Business

Technical Services	– Science-based Activities
	  Design-based Activities
	  Information Technology and Microelectronic Systems
	  Service Engineering

Production	– Construction
	  Agriculture
	  Horticulture
	  Forestry and Allied Industries
	  Manufacture
	  Craft-based Activities

Distribution	– Retail and Wholesale

Services to People	– Health and Community Care
	  Recreation Services
	  Media Industries
	  Hairdressing and Beauty Care
	  Performance Arts
	  Hospitality Services including Food and Accommodation
	  These modules can be studied in 3 phases
	  Introductory, Exploratory and Preparatory

Life Skills	

Personal and Career Development	– helps students to
	  match themselves to
	  future career possibilities

Industrial, Social and Environmental Studies	– understanding how modern industry works within society
Communication	– develops the ability to communicate effectively with people in different circumstances
Social Skills	– increases self reliance and the ability to get on with people
Numeracy	– learning how to use numbers and mathematical techniques in practical situations
Science and Technology	– understanding the role of science and technology and the practical use of scientific methods

Information Technology	– appreciation of the implications of
	  information
	  technology and 'hands on' experience

Creative Development	– encourages awareness of the student's own creativity and develops a critical sense
Practical Skills	– develops the use of practical skills and application to real tasks
Problem Solving	– identifying and solving 'real life' problems confidently

(Adapted from CPVE: *The Right Pegs in the Right Holes.* 1987. CPVE Unit, London)

Within this model all students are expected to study ten core areas as part of the CPVE programme, although additional studies such as GCSE, City and Guilds or RSA examinations may complement or replace some of the core areas. Again, the purpose of the core areas and additional studies is to provide a broadly-based course which includes access to information technology, problem solving, numeracy, life and communication skills. In principle the philosophy of CPVE is that it is school-/college-focused, student-centred and cross-curricular, often involving a consortium of institutions working together. As in a range of other programmes such as TVEI and B/TEC Foundation and First Courses, the concept of progression is a central ingredient both within the course and in enabling students to progress within further education and employment. In contrast with traditional forms of training which pigeon-hole students in particular occupations, CPVE provides students with the opportunity to sample areas of work not previously considered or available. An original feature of the course, again finding wider recognition in school and F.E., is the form of assessment commonly referred to as the Student Profile. Essentially the profile represents a record of achievement, or portfolio, which the student can show to prospective employers or education institutions. It is intended to provide a complete picture of the individual's achievements, over and above any qualifications gained. According to FEU (CPVE.9. 1986, FEU), 30% of students gain employment as a result of the CPVE course, with over 20% entering YTS courses and 10% being unemployed. In the circumstances, many CPVE students gravitate back into Further Education to take a number of courses such as B/TEC, CGLI, RSA and YTS, which are seen to be more vocationally oriented. Increasingly, this is the type of pattern which now characterizes CPVE progression.

B/TEC courses, though different in vocational emphasis and job relatedness, exhibit many of the 'integrative' features associated with CPVE and other related skills-based approaches.[6] Essentially B/TEC is an amalgamation of BEC and TEC, two separate bodies set up in the 1970s in response to the Haslgrave Report (1969), which recommended various reforms in Technical Education. In its statement *Policies and Priorities in the 1990s* (B/TEC, 1984) the Council did not accord any special or obligatory status to any subject.

> The place of subjects such as Communications, Economics, General Studies, Geography, Information Technology, Mathematics and Modern Languages . . . will be determined in the context of course aims, and not by reference to any merits of the subject in isolation . . . all B/TEC programmes of study have specific aims: achieving these aims is not just a matter of pursuing the specialism of the course; attention to knowledge, skills and understanding of wider relevance will also be required.

A noticeable feature of B/TEC is the emphasis which it places on mainstream studies and assignments rather than straight subject teaching.

In so doing, it actively encourages colleges to develop courses in conjunction with local employers, thereby identifying the knowledge and competencies that students need for work. Yet, despite the apparent vocational realism this supposes, it is interesting to note the high value placed on core 'social skills'. According to the joint Board '. . .self development skills, communicating and working with others, problem solving, decision making and investigating . . .' are seen to be key elements in *all* B/TEC courses. In the *Engineering Guidelines*, for example, the emphasis on social and communication studies is a central feature of the core skills involved (see Figure 1).

Figure 1   Core Skills

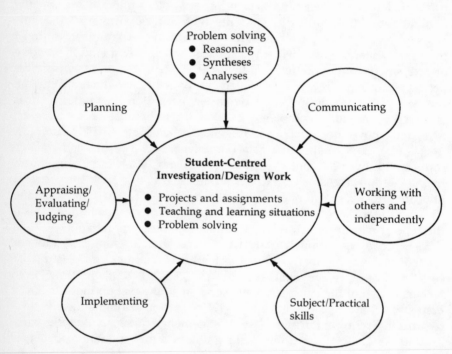

Reference should also be
made to appropriate
guidance on personal and
other general skills

(Adapted from *Liberal Education* No. 57, 1987 (Autumn))

A noticeable feature of the model is its lack of reference to specific knowledge *content*. Instead, the focus is upon common social skills and core themes to be arrived at by teachers working together in planning and teaching courses in an interdisciplinary way. According to B/TEC philosophy '. . .the process students engage in is often more important for common skills development than the product' (B/TEC, 1984). Perhaps not surprisingly the B/TEC requirement for common skills and core themes represents a radical change in teaching method, curriculum and INSET in many F.E. colleges and schools. The emphasis on 'integrative assignments', for example, has challenged specialist teaching and, alongside the integration of core skills across the curriculum, has influenced the way departments operate and teachers work.

Although different in orientation and focus 'integrative' courses, such as those associated with CPVE and B/TEC, are seen to have had a progressive effect on institutions (Radnor *et al*. 1986). Student-centred learning, cross-curricular development and school/college based initiatives have in many ways altered what Tipton (1973) refers to as the professional instrument-alism of traditional F.E. Yet in other respects contemporary further education and schooling have not proved as open and responsive as this view would seem to suggest. Despite evidence at the school and college level which demonstrates that teachers and students positively identify with CPVE and B/TEC courses, numerous problems remain. Lack of initial INSET and time to develop new initiatives has made it difficult for some teachers to adapt to the student-centred and cross-curricular orientation of B/TEC, TVEI and CPVE courses. Moreover, the limited resources made available to teachers working in time consuming areas associated with profiling, assessment and staff development have, during a period of financial cuts, hampered staff development at the school and college level. However, a more pressing concern has been the proliferation and duplication of pre-vocational courses converging together in the mid-1980s, all in competition for a declining cohort of school leavers. Such proliferation, despite efforts by the SEC and NCVQ to check it, has done little to achieve closer working relations between schools and colleges or alleviate confusion among parents, pupils and teachers about the status of such courses.

At present uncertainty abounds regarding two contradictory strands of government thinking about vocational education and training. On the one hand a variety of skills-based, cross-curricular and student-centred pre-vocational courses are being actively promoted, while on the other national curricular guidelines emphasizing subject teaching, testing and academic excellence are creating uncertainty at the local level. Despite claims that TVEI, CPVE and related pre-vocational courses have reduced divisive academic, technical and vocational distinctions in school and further education (Pring, 1985a), there is also evidence that such innovations have been accommodated and compartmentalized at the institutional level. In the case of TVEI, for example, while it has stimulated important discussions about progression, active learning and profiling, it has also anticipated major weaknesses in the National Curriculum. How, for example, does a prescribed curriculum of entitlement (*Better Schools*, 1985) square with school-based curriculum policy based on students' 'free' option choices? – even more problematic, how does student choice square with employer or parental choice? Perhaps not surprisingly, confusion remains over the concept of *progression*, with both *Better Schools* (1985) and the Education Act (1988) reinforcing 16 as the age at which formal education ends.

A number of additional changes are also occurring in Further Education which affect the progressive thrust of approaches associated with CPVE. The impact of NCVQ has been to secure the central place of employer-led qualifications, thereby reducing the significance of the *process* of further *education*. Moreover, as assessment becomes competency-based the danger is that the knowledge skills of educationists will be jettisoned for specific work skills demanded by employers. At present, the NCVQ stamp of approval appears to favour courses with work placements or work-based assessments. As a consequence, broader national objectives associated with CPVE and related school- and college-based courses, may not fit this employer-led remit. The signs are that employers will, for reasons of cheapness and convenience, recruit from those courses which are seen to deliver the skills they want, but without the educational frills. One consequence of such developments is that pre-vocational education is likely to become more stratified, with some pre-vocational courses gaining greater purchase on the job market than others. B/TEC, for example, is presently marketing its own courses, from First to National and Higher, as *the* major route into higher education and into a host of professional occupations associated with business, commerce, health and social services. Thus, despite the apparent progressive and integrated nature of B/TEC First and National Courses, there is little that is pre-vocational about them; essentially they are vocational in nature and marketed toward a particular ability range. One consequence is that little is offered to the middle ability range of 16–19 year olds, with even less on offer to low achievers whose involvement with pre-vocational foundation courses, such as LAPP and CPVE, at worst leads them nowhere and at best leads them into low status YTS courses. At the moment, as B/TEC and other boards jockey for NCVQ approval in order to ensure that they remain gatekeepers to the world of work, students whose general education is incomplete (or who have not decided on a particular occupation) are likely to lose out.

Thus, in returning to remarks made about Bernstein's work earlier on it would be a mistake to exaggerate either the challenge or ground that pre-vocational education has won in bridging theory and practice in education. From the outset there has been tension and resistance in the administrative structures of schools and colleges into which CPVE, TVEI and related courses have been introduced. In various ways State-sponsored privatization, associated with parental choice, assisted places, CTCs and opting out, have all strengthened the hand of central government, not least in undermining the advances that LEAs and local institutions have made in implementing pre-vocational education for all. In the circumstances, and following education cuts, falling rolls, reorganization and industrial action, it is perhaps not surprising that schools and colleges have adopted a cautious if not pragmatic approach to innovation. One consequence of this, coupled with government policy for NAFE, is that pre-vocational education will become accommodated within existing structures and pigeon-holed as a curriculum for less able youngsters. At one level, such categorization has been exacerbated by a lack of progression and accreditation of pre-vocational curriculum across the 14–19 age range, raising questions about the purchasing power of some pre-vocational qualifications in the labour market. At another, concern has been expressed about the close links now being forged between TVEI, YTS and CPVE, which reflects a growing tendency to target pre-vocational courses towards so-called unemployable students – despite 'official' claims that all three are designed for the whole ability range.

Following on earlier discussion about tripartism in further education and training, it is now possible to discern a growing pattern of differentiation across school and further education curricula, as shown in Figure 2.

Figure 2

14–16 (school)   16–18 (F.E./college)

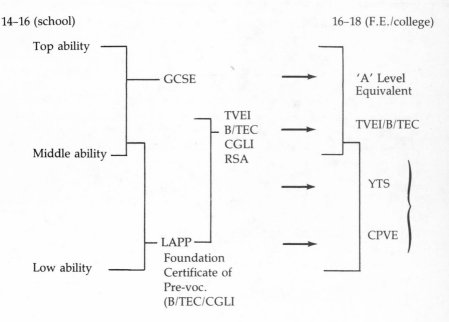

If such a model should be viewed with some caution, it nevertheless points to some of the broad types of banding now emerging in school and further education institutions. Such differentiation, of course, runs counter to the notion of progression associated with TVEI, CPVE and other pre-vocational courses, which were not originally designed to channel students in a predefined direction, but to accommodate the vocational needs of a broad ability range yet to make a decision about their future. By linking CPVE, TVEI, YTS, B/TEC, C and G and RSA courses, there can be little doubt that pre-vocational education does not represent an 'alternative route', but defines the direction by which young people progress into further education and the labour market. According to FEU (1986) there are disturbing signs that some colleges use courses such as CPVE to regulate the aspirations of low achieving recruits. Bowes (1987), for example, points to cases of students who have failed the entrance tests for pre-nursing, nursing and pre-residential care courses, being offered the CPVE course with an understanding that they would be reconsidered for these courses the following year. The inference is that, if they perform well on the CPVE course, they may achieve selection on the over-subscribed courses at a later date. This perception of CPVE as a selective feeder of 'less able' recruits into other programmes not only reflects back on the sink status of the course, but also raises further questions regarding race and gender issues. The FEU report, *Aspects of CPVE* (1986), has for example, highlighted particular areas of concern, with reference to the use made of CPVE as a selective feeder into nursery nursing and other courses by race and gender. The report comments on lack of recognition of multi-racial issues within CPVE curriculum, a criticism also raised by ALE (1986) in relation to B/TEC courses:

> It is thus a matter of some concern that, while the CPVE documents make passing reference to multi-cultural Britain, there is nowhere in the CPVE documents the central acceptance that would indicate and guarantee a positive recognition of cultural diversity and the issues attendant upon it . . . the use of the word 'bias' instead of 'racism' or even 'prejudice' does not adequately reflect the experience of young people in urban areas . . .

> (*Aspects of CPVE*, FEU, 1986)

Again, the issue of progression would seem important here. What students learn and where they progress to from CPVE, TVEI and B/TEC foundation courses has long-term implications, particularly if such courses become separated off from recognized and established courses at the school and college level. This point is aptly summarized by a CPVE student in a recent study: 'I think that I'm better prepared to start work, but not better prepared to get work' (Roberts, 1987). In theory, CPVE and courses like it offer students the opportunity to taste a range of possible work experiences, to enable them to make more realistic choices about work and further education. In practice, however, evidence indicates that many students remain 'contained' by low status pre-vocational courses (Green, 1986) and constrained by traditional ideas about suitable work for their age, sex, class and race (Bowes, 1987).

Vocational realism or idealism?

The rationale for pre-vocational education is that it contrasts sharply with traditional training and apprenticeship courses which explicitly induct school leavers into particular occupations. With the decline in manufacturing industry, followed by the break-up of the apprenticeship system and Industrial Training Boards, the ethos of craft training has gradually shifted away from job training and 'making things' to programmes designed to anticipate future changes in the labour market. From the late 1970s the collapse of work has not only seriously undermined traditional concepts of schooling and training, but it has also made it increasingly difficult to talk in any straightforward sense about the transition from school to work. Pre-vocational education represents an intervention in this process of transition seeking to offer a more flexible approach than 'time served' training allows. There is, however, more to it than this.

As the Conservative government acknowledges in its various official White Papers (see 1984, 1985), an important aim of pre-vocational education is that training for enterprise will somehow facilitate a shift to tomorrow's occupations encouraging inventiveness, entrepreneurial skills and the possibility of self-employment. Increasingly, this 'new' approach places high emphasis on economic awareness, learning by doing, self-reliance and adaptability, in the face of an imprecise and volatile labour market. In this respect, pre-vocational education closely mirrors the idealism of Conservative political and economic thinking: it is not simply something that follows on existing patterns of employment but *it is also part and parcel of the job creation process itself.*[7]

Thus, in contrast with the commonly expressed government view that the curriculum should emphasize greater vocational relevance, pre-vocational education approximates to, rather than reflects, the reality of the job market. In sociological jargon, it represents an approach paradigm which according to Cohen (1986) simulates issues in the 'real' world. With reference to the prevalence of role play games and simulation exercises he writes:

> This is a major educational growth industry at the present time largely thanks to the impetus given to simulation methods by the so-called 'active pedagogy' of the new vocationalism. Indeed, it is scarcely an exaggeration to say that CPVE is one big role-playing game in which students can practise everything from going for a job interview to setting up their own business by these means. At the same time, a whole youth culture has elaborated itself around 'Dungeons and Dragons' and similar fantasy games, based on the action maze principle. Here players take on a larger than life character drawn from medieval legends or science fiction, before embarking on a series of 'adventure modules' in which magic and violence usually 'rule OK'. These games are explicitly designed as an escape from the reality principles

modelled in educational simulations and are no doubt all the more popular and pleasurable for that. Yet the opposition between the two kinds of role playing is not always as clear cut as it might seem. To encourage a 16 year old boy who finds difficulty in reading and writing, to play at being his own boss is nothing if not to entertain his fantasies. But equally, if the same lad plays a 'thief' in a D and D scenario he may be closer to the practices of his everyday life, than his teachers would like to suppose.

Despite the apparent vocational realism employed in CPVE and related pre-vocational courses, there is little about the real world of work. Making young people flexible for a world without employment may perhaps explain why there is less emphasis on cognitive skills in the curriculum and more on 'life skills'. However, in these circumstances progressive aims associated with 'learning to learn' are likely to lose their meaning, the danger being that work becomes a subject in the curriculum like any other – something one learns about rather than something one does. The main paradox here again is not so much that there 'ain't no jobs', important though this may be, but that the *skills* associated with becoming a flexible worker have already been acquired at school, in the home and via young people's part-time experiences of work. Here the idea that pre-vocational education can somehow make young people ready for work, leisure or unemployment is presumptive: it fails to take into account the actual nature of the vocational experience and knowledge which they already possess.

Recognizing the failure of industry to provide adequate training, the Conservative government has transformed an essentially occupational problem into a 'skills' one, laying blame at the door of the schools and colleges for failing to deliver vocational realism. In praising its achievement in reforming mainstream education two government documents, *Training for Jobs* (1984) and *Better Schools* (1985) express the view that pre-vocational education represents an effective means of disseminating ideas about transferable skills, thereby altering young people's perceptions of industry, technology, work and mobility. In this respect, perhaps what pre-vocational education can do is influence positive attitudes toward careers in industry, trade and commerce. However, as a mechanism for actually skilling the major proportion of the labour force with productive skills pre-vocational education is a relatively weak mechanism. It is more likely that young people will learn the application of technical and applied skills at work, not within the framework of a school or college of further education. According to Senker (1986) this is not so much a criticism of school or F.E., but of government policy for failing to realize the relationship between off-the-job and on-the-job forms of training. With reference to the Japanese experience of schooling he writes:

> In a very real sense, the quality and effectiveness of Japanese vocational training results from the quality and effectiveness of the training which firms provide for managers and professional engineers . . .. Japanese 'failure' to

incorporate significant elements of technical education in school curricula does not seem to have detracted from their country's economic performance.

Notwithstanding evidence which indicates that TVEI, CPVE and other 'pre-vocational' initiatives have forced institutions to reconceptualize the processes through which young people are educated, this may be of little consolation to young people actually in search of work. In the wider society pre-vocational courses have the stigma of being second rate. Their credential value remains untested with employers, who tend to develop their own skills and aptitude tests in the selection of young recruits (Siggers, 1987). According to Atkins (1987) for all this vocational emphasis and hard won gain in pupil motivation, pre-vocational courses may well preclude school leavers from entering jobs with real economic power and status. This is not simply because such courses are 'new' or 'untested', but because they have emerged as separate from rather than integrated within recognized features of education, training and work. The point being made here is that if, for the majority of young people, a traditional subject-oriented curriculum is inappropriate to their needs and interests, it does not necessarily follow that pre-vocational education will compensate them for what they have missed out on. Again, if pre-vocational education is to have any impact it is essential that it should attract a cross-section of all young people, and not become a 'sink' subject for disaffected youth. Equally, it would seem important to generate careers for those encouraged to take them up via pre-vocational education, rather than as at present, leaving this side of the equation to the vagaries of the market mechanism. It is to this issue of progression across the links between school, college and work that the next chapter now turns.

Notes

1. Describing pre-vocational courses in such a global way has its dangers. Some courses are 14–16, some 14–18 and others, such as CPVE, are one year 16 + courses. It is also the case that while some B/TEC, C and G, RSA and other initiatives are *vocational* in emphasis, others are not. B/TEC foundation courses are, for example, pre-vocational in orientation, while B/TEC First Courses incorporate both vocational and pre-vocational concepts. B/TEC Nationals and Highers are noticeably vocational in orientation.
2. This is not to say, of course, that pre-vocational courses did not exist prior to NTI, e.g. Unified Vocational Preparation (UVP) (1976); 1979 YOP and related courses; 1980–81 CGLI '365'. MSC funded UVP and YOP before NTI (1981).
3. It should also be noted that pre-vocational courses intersect with one another, and with the more specifically vocational courses; for instance, CPVE is linked in extensively within TVEI and YTS, while in other respects it also acts as a feeder into YTS, B/TEC and related courses.
4. Also see Atkinson *et al.* (1986).

5. See Prais, S.J. and Wagner, K. (1985); Schooling Standards in England and Germany: *National Institute Economic Review*, No. 112.

6. In particular, B/TEC Foundation and First Courses (although see note 1, above).

7. A favoured view of Lord Young of Grantham.

Progression and Progressivism in TVEI

5

The Technical and Vocational Education Initiative (TVEI) is perhaps *the* major curricular innovation in schooling since the introduction of comprehensive education in the 1960s.[1] It represents a very real change in the ways in which schools are run, organized and funded. In a period otherwise characterized by cut-back and retrenchment in the education service, TVEI constitutes a novel if not paradoxical exception to the rule. There is today greater awareness of the large-scale influence of the project beyond its original pilot brief; alongside YTS and pre-vocational education initiatives such as CPVE, B/TEC, RSA, C and G and others, its imperatives for curricular and organizational change, its implications for staffing, resources, teaching relations and so forth, have reverberated throughout the educational system. Both in terms of categorical funding and delivery TVEI represents a distinct break with hitherto accepted models of curriculum development and reflects a 'new' approach to the ways in which government structures educational priorities at the local level. Following on as it does various 'crises' which beset schooling in the late 1970s, TVEI has emerged as a prototype for implementing educational policy and change. According to the Secretary of State for Education and Science, for example, the new City Technology Colleges (CTCs) will build upon the lessons of TVEI, both in terms of curricular planning and earmarked expenditure (DES, 1986a).

Despite its sudden arrival on the scene in 1983, TVEI has its roots in wider historical debate about the aims of schooling, not least in relation to the ways in which schools should respond to the needs of business, industry and commerce. TVEI then is not without controversy. On the one hand, its development reflects strong central government control which permits the intervention of the Training Commission's influence right down to the classroom level. Critics argue, for example, that this allows government to dictate the terms of the curriculum, thereby creating a narrow technical and vocational stream in the comprehensive school. On the other, TVEI supports local, technical and vocational education initiatives which in many cases are highly experimental, creative and long overdue. Those in favour of TVEI argue that historically deep-seated prejudice against technical and vocational education is élitist, and that any initiative which seeks to break down artificial barriers, between academic, technical and general knowledge in the curriculum, should be welcomed.

What constitutes TVEI and its extension beyond the original pilot phase varies widely across the country. Each LEA project differs in its institutional arrangements and model of implementation, depending on local perception, interpretation and circumstance. Yet, despite such variation, a number of principle aims and objectives are discernible, involving a commitment to:

- adopt a generic 14–16 core;
- equip young people to enter the world of work;
- offer equality of opportunity;
- provide real and/or simulated work experience;
- offer vocational options related to likely job opportunities;
- ensure balance between different curricular elements;
- provide a range of options and progression opportunities;
- develop active teaching and learning strategies;
- relate to other 14–18 provision including CPVE and YTS;
- initiate guidance, counselling and new forms of assessment.

(Adapted from *Supporting TVEI*, FEU, 1985)

From this brief outline it is apparent that TVEI is not so much a course as a programme designed to deliver change across the 14–18 age range. For this reason the terms 'technical' and 'vocational' should be interpreted broadly, to include a number of interrelated themes, issues and approaches. Essentially TVEI is not primarily concerned with subject teaching but with developing active teaching and learning strategies designed to complement existing practice in schools and colleges. Thus, in addition to promoting technology, business studies, personal and social education and so forth, TVEI has become synonymous with equal opportunities, mixed ability, profiling, guidance and counselling, accreditation, improved school/college collaboration, modular develop-ment, staff development and a host of other activities.[2]

Essentially, TVEI curriculum consists of a core, that is, a set of common experiences, options and modules very much in line with existing comprehensive education development. Core subjects normally include mathematics, English, science and physical education, which are part of the general school curriculum, and information technology, personal and social education, careers guidance and work experience, which have been introduced or enhanced by TVEI. Option blocks contain a set of subjects which can be freely chosen by students to meet their own individual needs. Some options have a more constrained structure which may include thematically grouped subjects, integrated subjects, or a modular programme arranged into complete units of study (Tenné, 1987). Evidence from the Trent Polytechnic TVEI Data Base (1986) indicates, for example, that more than 600 different subject titles were newly introduced to schools in the first three years of the Initiative, including business studies, technology, computing, information technology, creative and aesthetic studies, catering and many others.

The principal rationale of TVEI is that it should encourage young people to seek qualifications and skills which will be of direct value to them at work. In practice, a majority of students of TVEI programmes take examinations in established subjects which, as I will argue later, may or may not reflect positively on TVEI. However, evidence indicates that TVEI has led to some shift in students undertaking courses in technology and business studies (NFER, 1987). In this respect TVEI projects have had a positive effect in working with examination boards to establish new forms of curricula, accreditation and assessment strategies designed to accommodate active learning approaches. Thus in addition to GCSE, City and Guilds, RSA and B/TEC have now made inroads into school-based accreditation, incorporating non-examination areas associated with work experience, social skills, records of achievement and profiles.

Taking the initiative?

Amid much furore TVEI was hurriedly introduced into schools in 1983, following an announcement in Parliament in 1982. In a speech to the House of Commons (12.11.82) the prime Minister expressed' . . . a growing concern about existing arrangements for technical and vocational education provision for young people . . .', and asked the Chairman of the Manpower Services Commission, together with the Secretary of State for Education and Science, to develop the pilot scheme. Initially fourteen LEAs were selected to take part and, by 1985, participation in TVEI had increased to include the majority of local authorities. Evidence of TVEI's major size can be cited in the £250m budget allocated to it (with a further £900m earmarked for its Extension), in a period of falling rolls, cuts in public expenditure and schools reorganization. Perhaps, not surprisingly, the funds made available via TVEI proved irresistible to cash-starved LEAs and schools, despite the reservations expressed at the time by the teacher unions and educational establishments.

In essence the project may be viewed as an attempt at major innovation to stimulate curriculum development and to introduce new approaches to teaching and learning through a limited life project. Through the mechanism of categorical funding it is envisaged that the project will leave a permanent mark on secondary and further education. According to one observer 'TVEI represents one of the most significant developments in secondary education since circular 10/65, which heralded universal comprehensivization' (Dancy, 1984). However, as Chitty (1986) has pointed out, TVEI has been introduced by a Conservative government antagonistic toward comprehensive principles, not least in relation to their apparent failure to provide relevant technical and vocational education. In the past three decades, for example, schools have been criticized for being 'anti-industry' and for promoting academic values in the curriculum at the expense of technical and vocational skills. On this basis alone the claim that education should be made more relevant to vocational needs and aspirations of both pupils and society is compelling. Indeed, the argument that entrepreneurial culture should find its expression in the curriculum is, as Reeder (1981) maintains, not new; it has its origins in nineteenth century conceptions of schooling and is part of a 'recurring debate'. (See Wiener, 1981.)

More recently, with rising youth unemployment, schools have been subject to a period when the very ground rules of schooling have altered. The presence of the 'new sixth former' after ROSLA, for example, promoted thoughts about changing curriculum and teaching methods and has resulted in a plethora of pre-vocational courses in the 14–19 age range (B/TEC, CPVE and so forth). The centre of the most recent impetus for change could be seen in the dramatic collapse of the youth labour market in the late 1970s. This collapse meant that for most young people schools were no longer seen as the main transition or transmission point into a job at sixteen. Change in pupil destinations has itself promoted greater awareness within educational circles of the need to initiate widespread curricular innovation and reforms. Almost simultaneously a politically inspired debate about the purposes and practices of schooling has arisen. At one level, criticism has been directed at the apparent failure of schools to ensure a proper 'fit' between the vocational needs of young people in their charge and the requirements of the economy. At another, critics argue that the current obsession with vocational education and training is flawed and obscures a more fundamental problem, namely, 'that there ain't no jobs' (Bates *et al.*, 1984). However, as Dale has argued (1985) the significance of TVEI also relates to the prevailing political crisis which it was designed to address at the time. On the one hand, the content and orientation of schooling had to be changed; on the other, the process of changing schooling itself needed to be changed. From this viewpoint TVEI is not simply a barometer of the problems facing secondary education: it is also a strategic vehicle in influencing both the temperature and climate of schooling itself (Gleeson, 1987).

Since its inception in schools in 1983, TVEI has been the object of much controversy. At one level, debate has focused on the manner and mode by which the project has sought to inject greater vocational realism into the curriculum. At another, central government involvement in the running of schools and colleges, notably via MSC intervention, has drawn attention to wider changes in policy and decision making processes in education. In announcing the extension of TVEI (DES/DOE, 1986a) the government has effectively removed the 'pilot' status of the initiative and firmly replaced it with TVEI as the 'recommended' framework for mainstream national schooling 14–16. However, the 16–18 phase is still left to compete with YTS, the MSC's financially attractive 16–18 initiative (an issue taken up later). With a £900m budget over ten years, TVEI is clearly being promoted as a 'success' despite there being few evaluation results. This is especially true of the 16–18 phase which receives scant attention in the 1988 Education Act and which, again, makes little provision for the types of curricular experience and teaching relations being developed by TVEI and related pre-vocational schemes.

It is worth noting here that inherent in the extension proposals is the same hurried time-scale as experienced in the pilot projects. Despite the announcement of further large-scale funding for TVEI replication, LEAs are still experiencing government cuts in expenditure – school buildings in urgent need of repair, books and other essentials in short supply and teacher shortages in vital curricular areas. This, coupled with the after-effects of teacher action and the general low morale of the profession, will no doubt have an effect on the reception of TVEI extension in many schools and colleges.

The apparent 'success' of the pilot projects and the instruction given to LEAs in the extension documentation to base their submissions on 'the lessons emerging from the pilot TVEI projects', raises the question: What *are* the lessons of the pilot TVEI projects? In particular, what are the lessons for the least evaluated and reported phase of TVEI, the neglected post-sixteen element? Before looking at the specific issue of progression, it would first seem important to consider elements of TVEI in practice.

Policy and practice of TVEI

An important feature of TVEI is that it represents a four-year package, beginning at fourteen and progressing beyond the compulsory leaving age to eighteen. Within this programme, curricular coherence and progression towards nationally recognized qualifications constitute a major objective. Inherent in the initiative is co-operation between schools and colleges in the form of linked courses backed by coherent programmes and inter-institutional provision. However, before discussing TVEI further, it must be appreciated that TVEI is itself neither a universal nor, particularly as a process of innovation, a static thing. It varies widely across the country and each LEA project differs in its institutional arrangements and model of delivery depending upon the local perception and interpretation of the initiative (Gleeson and Maunders, 1985). As MSC itself concluded (in the 1984 TVEI Review), without criticism, the resulting projects were '. . . diverse' and '. . . responsive to local circumstances'. Such diversity and responsiveness within broad guidelines affected the content of TVEI in that '. . . activities vary considerably between projects, and to an extent, between colleges and schools within them'. Indeed, within each LEA project individual institutions often differ greatly in their approach to TVEI, depending on their traditions, aspirations and their perceptions of the initiative both at a national and local level.

Perhaps, not surprisingly, no neat or causal connection can be assumed to exist between the policy and the practice of TVEI. The caution here is against assuming that, for example, the MSC, LEA, employers, schools and colleges share a common viewpoint. At one level, the MSC may be interested in the extent to which its innovation has brought about a turnaround in the national curriculum; at another, the LEA may be more interested in managing the project and bringing about change in its schools and colleges, identifying its own influence on policy and so forth. At the school/college level practitioners may view TVEI in relation to their own particular institutions, localized problems, careers and so forth. Even if all three worked toward similar broad goals (there is some doubt about this beneath the rhetoric) perceptions vary in terms of the situations, priorities and problems experienced by different parties. One TVEI institution is different from another and the views of 'insiders' and 'outsiders' within each school and college influence perceptions. Moreover, different conceptions of reality held by interested participants within schools and colleges (e.g. pupils, teachers, parents) and outside them (e.g. LEA, employers, careers, MSC) will affect understanding of TVEI. Indeed, the majority of TVEI pilot projects have evolved to accommodate numerous internal and external changes in a variety of ways. Since 1985 emphasis on enrichment of the curriculum, teaching methods and assessment based upon learning by doing, problem solving and practical experience, has become more noticeable. However, this is perhaps not so surprising: most major curriculum development projects have a tendency to take on a momentum of their own over and beyond their original conception and in this respect TVEI is no exception. Hence, the question – What is TVEI? – must be answered in terms of place, time and circumstance (Gleeson and Maunders, 1985).

Within many LEAs and individual institutions there was an early assumption that TVEI constituted a technical and vocational thrust into the school curriculum, a thrust that aimed to alter traditional subject hierarchies ('the technicians' revenge'). This initial assumption has, however, proved to be unfounded as the 'bottom-up' nature of TVEI has ensured that rather than being a separate feature of comprehensive education TVEI now complements mainstream developments. According to Pring (1985b) not only has TVEI provided support for equal opportunities and teachers working with the full ability range, it has also drawn attention to coherence and progression in the curriculum. This can be interpreted in various ways. At one level, it refers to the importance of integrating work experience, careers, profiling and counselling into the mainstream of the curriculum. At another, it involves providing opportunities to build effective bridges between school, college and work.

Yet, if one attraction of TVEI is the financial and political support which it provides for a more vocationally relevant student-centred approach, the nature of that support has been felt by some to be divisive, challenging the ethos of comprehensive education itself (Wyatt, 1985; Golby, 1985; Fowler, 1985). Initial fears about the initiative have centred on arguments of tripartism linked with the vocationalizing of the school curriculum. Various critics argue that TVEI has led to a return of tripartism and selection which signals the destruction of the comprehensive system (Chitty, 1986; Golby, 1985). Others maintain that it is the potential narrowing and instrumentalization of the curriculum that causes the greatest concern. Dale (1985), for example, views TVEI as a political intervention 'unlike any other curriculum innovation we have seen before in this country'. Finn (1985) has criticized the 'New Vocationalism' movement and particularly recent MSC initiatives such as TVEI and YTS, citing their centralism as being non-democratic, ideologically-based and 'signalling the abandonment of equal opportunity as the central reference point of educational policy'. At the local level, contractual obligations entered into between LEAs and MSC, and the 'bidding' system encouraged by MSC for specific funding, have been criticized as divisive (Chitty, 1986). Moreover, the effects of centralized control, categorical funding and binding five-year contracts have radically altered LEA and institutional autonomy.

Thus, despite the rhetorical emphasis upon 'the broadening and enriching of learning opportunities', it is equally important, if not essential, to recognize the effect which TVEI has in re-organizing the environment in which such learning takes place. This question directs attention not only to what was there before TVEI came along, but also to the extent to which TVEI has brought in something different from previous curricular initiatives. Despite the refractory nature of TVEI, Gorbutt maintains that the project should not be viewed in isolation but as part of a well-defined drift towards redefining 14–19 education on more segmented lines (Gorbutt, 1984). In this respect TVEI is something more than 'innovation without change': it is linked with a broader movement to alter the shape and scope of comprehensive education despite its professed concern with mixed ability. This is a view endorsed by Evans and Davies (1987) whose case studies of four secondary schools and two colleges found that TVEI does little to lessen and, indeed, may exacerbate social and academic divisions between children inside schools and outside them. It is their contention that, while TVEI may have brought about a change in the content and organization of the curriculum for the 14–16 age sector, it has left largely untouched and undebated the broader context of schooling into which this innovation has been introduced. This, according to Shilling (1987), represents very real problems in terms of the ways in which teachers make sense of their professional role *vis-à-vis* other teachers. Participating schools and colleges have a contractual responsibility to recruit a balanced intake of students to TVEI courses. However, Shilling maintains that in many schools it is form teachers who have the eventual job of promoting TVEI to both sexes 'across the ability range'. What this recruitment structure does not allow for is that form teachers may be affected by a number of sources of influence, the effects of which do not coincide with this objective.

Thus, notwithstanding the positive effect which TVEI may have had in placing 'mixed ability' and 'equal opportunities' on the agenda, it has done little to address broader inequalities which find their expression in schools at the present time (Weiner and Millman, 1987). Moreover, recent evidence indicates that TVEI is skewed toward average and below average students (Tenné, 1987), with sex stereotyping persisting in choice of options, work experience placements and students' career intentions – a criticism endorsed in a recent national evaluation of TVEI (NFER, 1987).

> There was a clear sex differentiation in the type of work experience and activities undertaken by students. Most girls obtained placements in office work, community services, travel and tourism, personal services such as hairdressing, food preparation and related services such as hotel and restaurant work. In contrast, more boys than girls entered manufacturing, craft based and technical occupations, or had worked with electronics and computers. Work experience in retail and sales provided the most even distribution of boys and girls.
>
> (NFER, 1987)

When viewed alongside the subjects taken by TVEI students the NFER's findings confirm suspicions that TVEI does no more or no less to challenge existing inequalities in schooling despite the claims made of its 'success' (*Better Schools*, 1985). Figure 3 provides some insight into the subjects taken in 1985–86 by TVEI students of the 1984–85 intake in England and Wales.

Perhaps the greatest constraint in implementing change in schools and colleges, irrespective of the additional resources made available by TVEI, is the *time* factor. Developing cross-curricular initiatives which interrelate equal opportunities, profiling, modular studies, new forms of course work and assessment are labour intensive and tend to add extra pressure on already overstretched staff. This has been found to affect TVEI principles in a number of ways, not least in relation to teaching styles. From the starting point that TVEI schools have undertaken to make their courses practical and relevant to the world of work, what progress has been made in this direction? Based on preliminary evaluation work in six schools Barnes (1987) has looked at four key elements of TVEI practice, associated with

Figure 3 Subjects taken in 1985-86 by TVEI students of the 1984-85 intake in England and Wales

% of all boys/all girls

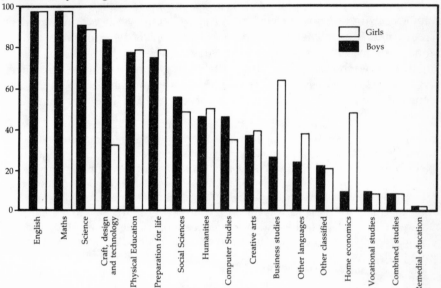

Adapted from R. Tenné (1987) *TVEI Students: Three years on* (TVEI Unit).

teaching styles, integration and what teachers say about 'negotiating' the curriculum. With reference to the latter, for example, Barnes observes that 'to make central decisions about pedagogy without involving affected teachers in the necessary rethinking is not likely to be a successful strategy'. Similarly, Harrison (1987) has commented that:

> Many teachers recognise the importance of problem solving activity but feel unconfident to promote it, sometimes perhaps assuming that, because the term has acquired a modern prominence, the process is a technical one alien to their normal capacity. There is a need for focused INSET to resolve this.

Certainly, there can be little doubt that the front loading of resources and lack of INSET in the 'early days' of the initiative has affected TVEI development throughout. The University of Leeds National Evaluation Report (1987) notes that the idea of technology in the curriculum has grown *ad hoc*, with a prevailing acceptance that it can be satisfied through 'bolt on' modules rather than integrated within the mainstream of the curriculum. Elsewhere, Saunders (1987) has observed a similar lack of planning and coherence with reference to work experience. The 'bridging' between education and work that the MSC and government have stressed in recent years is an aim manifest in the compulsory inclusion in each TVEI submission of a work experience element. Drawing on survey data collected in Spring 1986 from TVEI students in twelve LEAs, Saunders analysed their perspectives of work experience. Although many of the positive statements contained unqualified references to work experience as good or enjoyable, few contained any direct comparison with or references to school. According to Saunders, the data analysed suggests, overall, a positive yet complex picture. At present what government, employer or school considers worthwhile work experience (more conventionally referred to now as work based learning) is often at variance with what students think, a factor largely ignored in discussions about establishing closer links between school and work. However, in addressing this ignored dimension NFER (1987) has identified a number of broader criticisms of coherence in TVEI programmes.

> A sizeable proportion (40 per cent) of students felt that TVEI had turned out to be different from what they had initially imagined and for many of these, TVEI had fallen short of their expectations in some way. A similar percentage also thought that their TVEI schemes could be improved in some way. Students' disappointments with their schemes (and the suggestions made for change) often focused on inadequacies in existing schemes and classroom organisation. Teachers, it was felt, had not always known how to structure and run classes in which student centred learning methods were deployed. Planned activities and visits sometimes failed to materialise. Some students noted that there had been less access to new equipment than expected and that the completion of TVEI accommodation had been delayed. Other respondents mentioned that project work was not always adequately planned by staff, while others found it difficult to work on several projects simultaneously.

Inevitably the relative merits of TVEI will be judged in terms of what students think, a constituency sometimes overlooked in debates about the management and delivery of TVEI. Looking to the immediate future, the challenge to the project would seem to be two-fold. On the one hand, establishing closer links between key curricular elements within the programme, for example, remains a pressing concern. On the other, bringing coherence to bear in the emerging relations between modules, options, core curriculum and accreditation is a major issue yet to be resolved. The pressing issue is, therefore, one of effectively co-ordinating all the disparate elements of provision, so that teachers, pupils and parents know exactly where they stand in relation to the content of the curriculum, qualifications, career routes, and what is on offer in the colleges. Evidence to date suggests that there is confusion in the minds of some teachers, pupils and parents regarding how TVEI core elements (including profiling, work experience, etc.) complement the National Curriculum, GCSE, YTS City and Guilds, RSA, B/TEC, CPVE and other courses, which affects progression. Some would argue, however, that at least TVEI has addressed this issue, which hitherto had been ignored within mainstream schooling. In the circumstances, it would be naive to expect TVEI to have found 'answers' to all the problems raised. Viewed more realistically, the positive contribution of TVEI may be the way in which it identifies some of the limitations as well as some of the possibilities for implementing change.

However, as TVEI penetrates mainstream schooling variability is likely to be tempered with pragmatism, not least in relation to the imposition of a National Curriculum and organizational change on schools and colleges. If the guiding influence of government and MSC in such development is not immediately discernible their method of linking categorical funding with contractual delivery of curriculum is manipulative. In these circumstances LEAs can find themselves in the situation of doing the MSC's bidding, by encouraging schools and colleges to compete for a limited range of funds against a background of privatization and 'opting out'. The danger here is that for a number of reasons not all institutions compete for funds and resources on an equal footing, particularly in terms of falling rolls, catchment and resources. One consequence of this is the phenomenon whereby institutions feel compelled to throw themselves at innovation, without thinking through the longer-term implications. Modularization is but one case in point. As a recent advocate of modular programmes has pointed out, if such a programme '. . .is not underpinned by dramatic and radical change in the mode of delivery then it is merely the same drivel packaged differently' (Newman, *TES* , 29.11.85). Moreover, the James Report's (1972) observations on over-teaching in schools confirm criticism of excessive over-direction by the teacher in circumstances where pupils have too few opportunities to learn for themselves (DES, 1985). According to Lewis (1986) achieving such 'meta-goals' (learning by doing, learning how to learn and so forth) is not a straightforward activity. He argues that it is far easier to talk about the aims associated with 'co-operation not competition' in the curriculum than to implement them in practice. The point being made here is that method is no guarantee of quality or delivery at the school level. The teacher in innovative situations still has to balance the social/motivational gains against apparent academic loss. The irony is that teachers, having become more formal after the progressive era of the sixties and seventies (when progression was blamed for falling standards), are now being asked to change track again. Willis (1984) dismisses such development as intended to bring children 'into the safe camp of conformism'; elsewhere Hargreaves (1982) restates the danger that the modern teacher may not address the *whole class* as frequently but will say 'the same thing thirty plus times to individuals' (Lewis, 1986).

The point has been made, not least by teachers themselves, that the content and experience of TVEI is not original – elements such as negotiated curriculum, vocational courses, work experience, modular curriculum and so forth, have all existed to some degree within mainstream education. What is perhaps 'new' is the speed at which centralized control of education and training has occurred, and the influence which the MSC now exerts over colleges (via YTS) and schools (via TVEI). Developments within the further education sector, such as the

Unified Vocational Preparation Scheme (1976), prefigure a greater expansion of the 'new Vocationalism' via the Youth Opportunities Programme (YOP), and later YTS and TVEI (1983). Yet, in other respects, TVEI is itself neither a universal nor, particularly as a process of innovation, a static or determined thing. The variability of TVEI nationally derives from its original and apparently 'bottom up' design in which (while broad national criteria and guidelines have been established), the detailed curricular planning and implementation have been left in local hands. For whatever combination of reasons, once they had agreed to participate first round schools and colleges had to decide how best to approach the new, as yet not fully understood, undertaking. Murray Saunders (1985) has used three broad categories to indicate how schools generally responded to TVEI:

1. Adaptive Extension: A strong interpretation of TVEI – it has been used to change the whole curriculum.
2. Accommodation: TVEI adapted to fit the general shape of the existing curriculum structure.
3. Containment: TVEI absorbed by the existing school pattern.

The danger of placing individual schools at a single point somewhere along such an Adaptive Extension to Containment continuum is that such a model is too static to convey the degree of past movement or future intentions. Moreover, while it may be argued that the initial approach of the individual Project schools varied from Adaptive Extension to Containment, there was, at first, a *universal* need to see how far TVEI could be 'accommodated' within the demands of the existing school organization and curriculum. These demands were themselves realized against the immediate background of falling rolls, reorganization and later industrial action. Initial attitudes were also conditioned by the early perception of the Initiative as a technical and vocational, theme-led project. For example, an apparent early accent on technical and craft resources led some staff in this area of the curriculum to welcome what they saw as a redress of school priorities away from 'academic' to technical subjects.

The fact that TVEI/MSC policy can be seen to by-pass conventional DES/LEA channels is not necessarily felt by teachers to be the main issue. To them the 'by-pass' may be seen to indicate government intention to impose its will on schools and colleges at a time of falling rolls and industrial action. In less conspiratorial fashion there are those who argue that the project's positive commitment to mixed ability, experiential learning, equal opportunities, special needs and so forth complements rather than contradicts comprehensive principles and, if anything, strengthens democratic participation in education at the present time. McCulloch (1987) argues, for example, that the utilitarian rhetoric and objectives that accompanied the launching of the initiative have been *subverted* via their incorporation into mainstream education. Although

TVEI may have been successfully established in the context of Thatcherite politics at the national level it may yet, at the local level, give way to a revival of more liberal notions of educational practice. According to McCulloch it is easy to interpret TVEI as just the latest in a line of attempts by employers to perpetuate traditional social and work patterns at the expense of working class children. While it may be that TVEI emanates from particular historical ideals and attitudes identifiable as a conservative tradition, it is naive to draw simplistic conclusions on that basis. McCulloch argues that both the character and extent of TVEI's influence remain open to question and dispute. Whether or not TVEI or other forms of technical initiative maintain a narrow vocational bias is not historically predetermined. For McCulloch technical and vocational education will continue to be inextricably linked with wider social and political factors, as an avenue of conflict over the nature of British Society. As such, the content and form of technical and vocational education remains contested rather than given.

From this viewpoint TVEI is not necessarily seen as a divisive force arriving out of the blue, but as a *catalyst* which may accelerate changes in schools, which are already there in actual or potential form. It may be that this view of TVEI stretches the chemical analogy too far. A chemical catalyst promotes or accelerates a process without itself being changed and, in this sense, it could be taken out of the resulting product in its original form (Gleeson and Maunders, 1985). The first part of the analogy – the agent promoting change – may be appropriate for the purposes of evaluation but the second part would direct attention away from the possible interactive nature of the catalyst itself – which, in the case of TVEI has implications for the issue of replicability. In other words, might the system revert to its original form once TVEI is taken out? (Owen, 1984). If to date there is no strong evidence that centralism has either strengthened or weakened comprehensive principles, it is in the post-16 phase of TVEI that there is a real danger of the re-emergence of tripartite divisions. Ranson *et al.* (1986), for example, argue that:

> What has almost been eliminated from secondary education is now re-appearing at tertiary level with Advanced levels forming a more entrenched grammar stream, TVEI . . . indicating a technical track, with YTS comprising the new tertiary modern sector.

In view of the national extension of TVEI and the general firming up of vocational qualifications via NCVQ, there can be little doubt that tripartism will percolate across the 14–19 curriculum. The subject of tripartism is also central to the return of selection, privatization and the rise of City Technology Colleges (CTCs). If, at one level, the proliferation of pre-vocational education and training courses such as TVEI, YTS, CPVE, B/TEC and CTCs has introduced a veneer of choice and variation into the system, at another, little is known about the effects of such initiatives on student progression beyond 16. In view of TVEI's commitment to bridge school, college and work, it would seem important to consider this neglected area of debate.

Staying on: 16–18 progression in TVEI

One of the fundamental concepts of TVEI is that it is a 14–18/19 initiative. Those embarking on a TVEI scheme at fourteen are 'expected' to remain within that scheme until eighteen and, as a planned and well-resourced 14–18 initiative, TVEI reasonably may have been expected to increase 'staying-on rates' post-sixteen. However, national figures (MSC/NSG, 1986b) show that 'staying-on rates' in full-time education, for the first TVEI cohort to reach this stage, were, to say the least, varied. 'Win some, lose some', reported the *TES* at the time. Some schools and some LEAs managed to increase their staying-on rates significantly, others experienced disappointingly low rates and many found no significant change at all. From early information, a similar situation appears to have occurred in the 'second round' LEAs and the second cohort in first-round authorities who began their post-sixteen phase in Autumn 1986. To many, this apparent failure of TVEI is seen as a damning criticism. However, it must be said that in many projects early cohorts of TVEI students experienced little to suggest that these rates might change, mainly due to the bottom-up, front-loaded nature of pilot projects and the rapid implementation of TVEI. Moreover, the statistics are dealing with a comparatively small sample of 'selected' pupils and, as such, are particularly vulnerable to distortion.

The significance of the number of TVEI 'arrivals' post-sixteen is one that cannot be over-emphasized at a time of falling rolls, school reorganization and increased competition. Post-sixteen, schools and colleges are geared to 'numbers' and when insufficient students arrive to form specific groups/courses, all but the most imaginative of institutions experience difficult decisions and institutional problems. This has been the experience of many schools and colleges involved in TVEI over the past year and must be seen as problematic in a planned 14–18 initiative in years to come (Gleeson and Smith, 1987).

In seeking to establish the influencing factors behind staying-on rates and, indeed, pupil destinations generally, a number of areas of influence may be identified and related to practice: the school, the college and the 'ecological' . . . environment, historical and economic influences, social and cultural background . . . and so forth (Eggleston, 1977). In terms of the ecological it is suggested that the immediate and specific influences of a pilot curriculum project like TVEI may be considered as marginal to the long-term economic and sociological trends of 'ecology' in an area. None the less possible short-term attitudinal and organizational influences which might be effective in changing the pattern are a neglected area of evaluation. With the extension of TVEI developments into mainstream schooling the need for such further evaluation would seem pressing. In terms of the school the initial perceptions and reactions concerning TVEI entry and the way in which they have influenced the management, planning, allocation of resources, staff attitudes and actions, are discussed in detail by Saunders (1985) and are reported on by HMI (1985), NFER (1987) and others. These reports confirm that the influences of the school are complex, varied and interrelated. They have, as their background, the political, the 'ecological', the 'culture' of pupils (Willis, 1977), the traditions and 'ethos' of the school (Rutter *et al.*, 1979) and the attitudes and experiences of staff. It is against this background that the factors affecting destinations of pupils post-sixteen must be viewed.

When considering the influence of the school on pupil destinations the focus often falls on the amount of liaison between schools and colleges, their relationships and traditions, staff attitudes and personal experiences. These may be expressed through the 'hidden curriculum' and in guidance given throughout the school. There is ample evidence from local TVEI evaluation reports that these factors are prevalent and influential in schools within TVEI projects. However, this appears to have been an area neglected by the planning process in many projects. A further area related to attitudes, perceptions and aspirations within projects and individual institutions is that of the curriculum *content* provided and its coherence within post-sixteen provision. This will affect the 'bias' of the project, largely dictate the ability and gender spread and influence institutional liaison, providing a further area of influence for pupils post-sixteen. Relating directly to this is the issue of the selection of pupils for TVEI participation within institutions which may prove to be a significant influence on 'destinations' statistics (Evans and Davies, 1987). However, in terms of national replication this may not be as contentious an area provided that all pupils share the TVEI experience.

The curriculum content of individual schools and its coherence with post-sixteen provision provides evidence of further neglect in many cases and yet is a vital area of influence for pupils deciding on post-sixteen destinations. In many schools the initial model of TVEI provision has been one of 'containment' (Saunders, 1985); curriculum change is often minimal, the introduction of 'vocational' qualifications (C and G., B/TEC, etc.) often rejected, and coherence with much of the F.E. provision therefore minimized. However, in maintaining traditional school structures in this way, a continued coherence with sixth form provision has been continued. In other schools the reliance on 'low-level' provision for TVEI has ensured that none of the vocational 'goats' were mixed with the academic 'sheep' (Golby, 1985) and hence there has been little coherence or provision at sixth form level. The solution to this problem of 'Fixing the Mix' (Evans and Davies, 1986) can only be if there is no mix to fix and that

TVEI extension has a 'whole-school' approach with corresponding coherence of provision for all ability levels post-sixteen. If it is to succeed, TVEI must not be used as a device to placate and control the average to less able while allowing the high flyer to pursue the traditional academic and prestigious route.

An often-expressed reason for low numbers in TVEI 16–18 is the attraction of YTS with its employment potential and financial incentive. It is ironic that in a planned 14–18 initiative now being extended throughout the country and promoted as being a 'success' by MSC, the same government 'QUANGO' should be promoting its other 16–18 'success' – YTS – and positively discriminating in its favour by offering payment to participants. For many TVEI youngsters there is no option of staying in full-time education and completing their TVEI programme when faced with the financial attraction of YTS, or the fact that some industries recruit only through YTS The MSC (*TVEI Review*, 1985) partially touched on this issue by suggesting that a progression into YTS is acceptable 'in cases where YTS is the only route to a particular industry'. In any other case YTS is seen as 'not normally the route of progression which TVEI intends'. Paradoxically, this same body claims to be pursuing a policy of rationalization of education and training 14–18. There are now links between YTS and CPVE (via the 'alternative route') and moves to introduce more nationally recognized qualifications into YTS via NCVQ. The signs are that TVEI has become hooked into this equation which, again, raises interesting questions about the meaning of the term progression.

In looking at the issue of 'numbers' and TVEI 16–18, as with schools, 'ethos', staff attitudes, experiences and perceptions and the 'ecology' of the area, are all background influences within which actions must be viewed. Add to this the 'special' nature of F.E., in terms of legal status, entrepreneurial spirit and establishment structure, based on the 'points' system referred to and course gradings, and it is within this context that the entry of TVEI into the post-sixteen sector must be considered.

The post-sixteen TVEI experience is as varied as TVEI 14–16 and has been delivered in a variety of ways. School sixth forms, sixth form colleges, tertiary colleges, colleges of further education, agriculture and horticulture have all been involved, as have other specialist provisions such as TVEI centres and establishments of higher education. In most projects, local colleges have formed part or all of the provision post-sixteen and have often had an involvement pre-sixteen within a variety of linked provision. However, many difficulties have been experienced in the area of linking institutions where there are differences of funding, administrative structures, payment and conditions of service and qualifications of staff. Some further examples of organizational considerations which have affected colleges are outlined by McCabe (1986) and discussed in more detail later:

Within a college, there is eagerness to be involved in the project but some concern as to how TVEI's specialist requirements could be met without distorting the complex programmes of a large interlocked organisation. If TVEI students, individually, could be 'slotted into' already existing programmes it would be simple enough . . ..

TVEI requirements add the complications of more intensive tutorial guidance and record keeping plus an 'enhanced' programme – one principal has estimated that to accept about 70 students, who would have come to college in any case, on TVEI terms would represent an extra work load equivalent to three or four lecturers plus some timetable reorganisation.

This is perhaps the main stumbling block for colleges as they may feel that their commitment would have to be estimated and underwritten in advance before the implementation of TVEI. A further problem to college departments is that '. . . there is, it is said, no slack in college staffing – in new technology areas, for example, there may already be many students and not enough staff while other courses depend on a considerable proportion of part-time staff' (McCabe, 1986). This could be a serious problem, for in the very areas that TVEI is promoting (new technology, business studies, food and related services, etc.) many colleges are already operating at capacity.

In many post-sixteen college situations there is a vision of the project being planned by 'school-oriented people' and an apparent assumption of minimal change on the basis that 'we already provide technical and vocational education'. In some cases this has led to a lack of interest in the preparation of courses to accommodate the prospective TVEI clientele. This attitude is reinforced by the views of many post-sixteen staff who feel that they provide appropriate courses anyway and that if TVEI students enter courses of their choice, leading to nationally recognized qualifications, then all is well and no change is needed. A further assumption is that TVEI only provides colleges with the students that they would have had anyway (Gleeson and Smith, 1987).

In striving to achieve a coherent programme 14–18 the 'drop-out' rate at sixteen has been, and is, an important factor for post-sixteen institutions involved in pilot projects. However, these same institutions must also look to their own responses to the initiative when questioning the coherence, progression and numbers staying in the project. The situation is now changed somewhat and for institutions preparing for involvement in TVEI replication (where it could be that all their feeder schools are providing a TVEI experience for their students), the importance of creating a planned, coherent progression and maximizing staying-on rates at a time of falling rolls and increased competition is an opportunity that cannot afford to be missed.

The point at issue is that TVEI is a 14–18 initiative and, as such, should be planned by *all* institutions involved, from the beginning. It has been suggested that in certain projects this joint planning has been minimal and that the projects were planned with little input from the post-sixteen sector, especially F.E. Any such lack of integrated planning may result in a fragmented project, lacking coherence, and hence not providing a 'natural progression' for students involved. This, in turn, is likely to have an effect on staying-on rates and involvement in TVEI post-sixteen. By not involving F.E. at an early stage in the planning process, as an equal partner, not only is the chance of coherence minimized but considerable expertise is also lost. This has particular significance for the planning of TVEI replication.

According to FEU (1985):

> Colleges will wish to ensure the status both of their contribution to the planning process and of the new development within the college by allocating staff of the appropriate seniority and experience to the planning groups. They must also be concerned to stress the cross-departmental nature of such developments.

One of the implications of this statement is that the *co-ordinator* of any TVEI project within an establishment must have the necessary status, time and experience to plan, co-ordinate and develop a cross-curricular initiative involving changes in curriculum content, learning strategies and teaching styles. This co-ordination will, of course, not only involve one institution but often a whole consortium. The need for status and the 'institutional clout' associated with it is one issue that has been identified in pilot projects (NFER, 1985). Indeed the status afforded to the co-ordinator within an institution is often seen as a reflection of the priority placed on the project by the management of that institution. It has been suggested above that the issue of priority and status afforded to TVEI by the post-sixteen sector and by others in the initial planning of TVEI is an important factor in the 16–18 debate. It is here and in the area of planning a coherent progression 14–18 that the future of the 16–18 neglected area lies.

One area of school and college contact where coherent planning could begin is the link course. It is suggested (FEU, 1985) that F.E. will have to rethink the rationale of link courses and review the relationship between existing provision and TVEI requirements in seeking to plan a coherent progression 14–18. Much existing link course provision is seen as in direct contrast to this and the views of 'consumers' of link courses often reflect a negative influence in terms of progression and coherence. Indeed, a view expressed by some F.E. staff is that link courses actively discourage participation in post-sixteen education.

In some projects link courses are seen to fall into this category, with few being specially designed for TVEI. Many of these courses use part-time F.E. staff and are based in schools or annexes and by the nature of their certification ensure an 'average' ability clientele. Further, there is often no recognized progression to many link courses. This has been confirmed by students in post-sixteen TVEI, who were link-course 'graduates', the same students often reporting repetition and duplication of work in their first year at college. This must be viewed as a major area of concern, for if TVEI students can see no apparent and obvious progression in their 14–18 programme, it is hardly surprising if they leave that programme at sixteen or seventeen. However, this is not the case in all colleges and it is suggested that successful link course provision and school/college consortia arrangements may form a sound basis for initial TVEI programme planning. Many colleges have established a successful and impressive array of link-course provision, utilizing resources to the full and thereby avoiding costly duplication. It is suggested that it is upon this type of relationship that TVEI links should be established and a planned 14–18 progression developed.

Much of the debate in and around link courses is concerned essentially with the status and priority given to them and with who attends the courses and why. School teachers tend to feel that F.E. staff have an 'instrumental' approach and are critical of the priority that link courses are afforded. F.E. staff, on the other hand, are critical of schools and often feel that link courses are used by schools to accommodate the less able and 'problem' students. However, most of these criticisms tend to be founded on misunderstandings of the problems, difficulties and conditions of the criticized. This, of course, is an all too common problem within education but is especially ominous in a 'planned' 14–18 initiative linking schools and colleges in what should be a coherent four-year progression. In terms of the school-to-college transition and staying-on rates these attitudes must be influential.

Clearly, what is needed is a planned, coherent system of link-course provision within TVEI, offering pupils a clear progression post-sixteen. Status and priority of provision must be ensured within the project and institutions and their programmes must accommodate the whole ability range. Since TVEI is essentially an integrated scheme, liaison between institutions and the development of understanding between schools and F.E. should be afforded priority in any project. Better inter-institutional co-operation will develop only through contact, involvement and communication at all levels in the initial overall planning of TVEI, in curriculum and staff development and in assessment and evaluation of TVEI.

In many of the pilot projects the development of sound inter-institutional relations are being fostered through the meeting of all collaborating institutions. These meetings are varied and numerous, involving senior management and classroom teachers in planning, developing, administering and evaluating their projects. All the indications are that such meetings are beneficial, and it is suggested that time devoted to such liaison must be considered a worthwhile investment of TVEI funds. One project, for example, reports 'some encouraging signs of an emerging new relationship between schools and the FE college, a relationship which simply did not exist prior to TVEI' (McCabe, 1986).

Bridging the compulsory to post-sixteen education 'time-gap' has proved a further area of concern within some projects, as has the enrolment of TVEI pupils by individual colleges where a school-to-college transition has occurred. In certain pilot projects, following initial correspondence and interviews, there has often followed a period of up to three months where no contact between the Project and the student has been made. It is felt by staff involved that this period has contributed to numbers of 'intending' students never arriving at the post-sixteen phase. Clearly, in a 14–18 continuum this gap must be bridged in order to minimize these transitional difficulties. This experience highlights the administrative difficulties that may be faced post-sixteen and points to the need for a planned policy to bridge school and college, thereby maximizing staying-on rates in post-sixteen TVEI.

At the commencement of the post-sixteen phase, further complications have been experienced. One central issue revolves around numbers and the use of 'infill' to make viable TVEI groups. This poses the question; Who is a TVEI student? Is it a person who has followed a TVEI course for two years 14–16 and then transferred to the 16–18 phase to attend an appropriate course which is *not* designated as being TVEI-related? Or is it someone attending a designated TVEI course who has not previously followed a TVEI course at 14–16? Either way, this situation poses problems in an initiative designed on the basis of a coherent progression 14–18. Often the majority of students on 'TVEI courses' post-sixteen are 'infill' students who have not followed a TVEI programme previously. This situation makes a nonsense of curricular links 14–18 and the continuity and progression implicit within TVEI. To further compound the problem, students' experiences of TVEI pre-sixteen often vary so greatly as to make any notion of coherence and progression 14–18 impractical with the first cohort. MSC (*TVEI Review*, 1985a) acknowledges these difficulties by suggesting 'induction' courses for this type of 'infill' student, 'to enable new entrants to gain maximum benefit from the last two years of the four-year programme'. This situation could, of course, change with the general replication of TVEI within LEA areas. Dependent upon local arrangements, large numbers of students entering post-sixteen education will have experienced TVEI provision. The challenge is then for the post-sixteen sector to provide the appropriate experiences leading to nationally recognized qualifications and further progression across the whole ability range and across their total 14–18 provision.

For post-sixteen TVEI based in school sixth forms some of the problems concerning continuity of provision mentioned above are lessened. On the other hand, problems of appropriate course provision in a comparatively limited curriculum are increased unless local institutions of F.E. are used in a consortia of provision. This, however, raises a number of issues in and around student numbers, tertiary reorganization and academic entrenchment which affect perceptions, decisions and, ultimately, the kind of TVEI provision that such institutions can offer to the whole ability range. The issue of 'ownership' of students is one such issue, especially when institutions are operating within a consortium of post-sixteen provision. Indeed, this is a prime consideration for many institutions faced with reorganization and falling rolls.

One universal panacea for many of the problems associated with appropriate course provision has been the use of the Certificate of Pre-Vocational Education (CPVE). Although this may be seen as highly appropriate by some, it must be acknowledged that CPVE is only a one-year course and has in many cases reduced TVEI to a three-year initiative. For students who entered the 16–18 phase and TVEI/CPVE, many are moving out of TVEI after three years; in some cases after their institutions had not accepted them on courses of their choice at 17 +. This raises the issue of selection for courses within the post-sixteen sector and the perceived 'value' of TVEI and CPVE to those who are selecting students for such courses. What price progression in these circumstances?

Is there life after TVEI?

Following publication of three significant White Papers: *Training for Jobs* (1984), *Better Schools* (1985) and *Working Together* (1986) it is evident that TVEI can no longer be viewed simply as a pilot scheme with a short life expectancy. With the nationwide 'replication' of TVEI announced in 1986, it is clearly being promoted as a 'success' alongside other 'reforms' outlined in the 1988 Education Act. The main implication of TVEI extension is that TVEI and its philosophy will become part of British mainstream education. As a consequence, MSC will have a major stake in the compulsory sector of education to complement their already large stake in post-sixteen education and training via Work Related Non-Advanced Further Education (WRNAFE), the Youth Training Scheme (YTS) and the Employment Training Programme (ET). Although there is little evidence to date of MSC using its 'muscle' in these areas it is obvious to many involved that a certain degree of muscle flexing is taking place. Further, when areas of MSC activity such as the Training Standards Advisory Service (TSAS), and the National Council for Vocational Qualifications (NCVQ) are considered, the enormity of their involvement becomes apparent and the fears of centralized control seem to be very real. These moves are highlighted when one reads that the job details for the TSAS clearly state that MSC's new YTS 'inspectorate' may be operational in other areas of MSC involvement, including school and F.E. However, such a pessimistic view must be set alongside a familiar question regarding funding curriculum projects: What happens when the money runs out? The level of funding for TVEI extension is, for example, far less generous than for the pilot project.

If one of the anomalies about the pilot project is that it focused on a relatively small pupil cohort, another is that it created discrepancies in staffing and resources within and between schools. The hope that government policy designed to extend TVEI will rectify such anomalies is unlikely to succeed, not least because the level of funding is inadequate to meet the needs of the majority of institutions to be involved. With reference to 16–18 provision, for example, the signs of neglect are already there. Within TVEI projects there has been wastage of resources, particularly early on in the project, due mainly to the rapid 'front-loaded' nature of the funding, which has resulted in a failure to even consider planning and resourcing 16–18 provision in many areas.

The lack of planning, difficulties in achieving a coherent curricular provision and 'structural' problems within projects and individual institutions are just some of the factors that have combined to make many of the first attempts at post-sixteen TVEI somewhat difficult. Others revolve around what is emerging as the key issue in 16–18 TVEI pilot projects: *numbers*. Low numbers combined with a lack of curricular coherence have led to a situation in many schools and colleges where TVEI post-sixteen is almost non-existent. Competition from traditional courses and the attraction of YTS are blamed by many for this situation although other factors, including the underfunding of pre-vocational education, are primary factors. While it may be the case that TVEI has been nudging for reform post-sixteen it is doubtful whether it alone will be enough to succeed. However, TVEI is only one of the major challenges facing the post-sixteen sector in the immediate future. The requirements of WRNAFE are already making an impact on F.E. colleges as are new YTS demands. GCSE, A/S levels and CPVE are beginning to initiate qualification-led change in both schools and colleges and corresponding curriculum change will be required by TVEI. The forthcoming National Vocational Qualifications (NVQ) framework will be fully operational by 1991 and, by introducing competency-based assessment into a restructured national system, will demand radical changes in curriculum content, methods of delivery and assessment procedures. It is the combination of these challenges that will undoubtedly change the post-sixteen sector. These changes will require an appropriate staff development programme which, in turn, will entail institutional development.

In terms of the changes required to provide an appropriate TVEI experience within a framework of nationally recognized qualifications, an inter-institutional curriculum will need to be examined. Any such change will also need to be set against the background of TVEI aims and criteria. In practice these challenges have been met in a variety of ways through the development of new courses, the 'enhancement' of existing provision, the 'bolting-on' of TVEI elements to conventional courses and the use of 'similar' courses such as CPVE – in some cases all within one institution. One model that appears to be particularly appropriate to post-sixteen provision is that of a TVEI 'core' within existing, nationally recognized and prescribed qualifications which have been suitably enhanced. To operate fully with TVEI a college would need not only to provide all of these 'enhancements' but also to build into its programmes special tutorial arrangements and profiling/record of achievement to ensure continuity from school. A certain degree of control as to who does what in terms of course provision would also be necessary.

Further, curricular change is required at the post-sixteen phase to accommodate innovation and developments taking place 14–16. Developments such as modular provision will need to be responded to by colleges in terms of linked courses/modules and generally by the post-sixteen sector in terms of progression. The move towards more active approaches to learning now taking place in schools as a result of TVEI, and in response to GCSE, will need careful consideration in terms of progression and the provision of a coherent 14–18 continuum. Already there are signs that, within TVEI, students in their first year post-sixteen are reporting duplication of provision and a more didactic approach in teaching method than they experienced within TVEI at school. This, in some cases, has led to their leaving the post-sixteen TVEI programme and opting for the more practical work-based YTS.

Explicit within TVEI is that work experience is a compulsory element of every programme: 'The construction of a bridge from education to work is begun earlier by giving young people the opportunity to have direct contact and *planned* work experience with local employers in the relevant specialisms' (MSC 1986a). According to MSC, work experience should be *planned and appropriate* and be an integral part of TVEI programmes (MSC, 1986b). Although many post-sixteen courses of study contain some element of work experience, leading to the comments of 'we already do this', it is suggested that many such courses do not see this experience as part of an *integrated* course element as demanded by TVEI and that contrary to the belief of many, especially in F.E., this constitutes a neglected area within the post-sixteen provision of TVEI.

Experiences of TVEI within the post-sixteen sector indicate that without the appropriate joint planning and delivery, together with sufficient curriculum and staff development, it is difficult to provide a coherent TVEI programme and ensure that the MSC's 'aims', 'criteria' and 'content of programme' are implemented. Many of the problems experienced in the early years of TVEI post-sixteen are felt to be due to lack of initial planning, curriculum and staff development and 'institutional difficulties'. Others may arise from the management structure, size, status and traditions of institutions and consequent perceptions of, and status afforded to, TVEI. The organizational form of an institution has a major influence on determining the actions and attitudes within that establishment. Schools and colleges may, for example, experience difficulties in implementing an initiative such as TVEI, which is cross-curricular, within a rigid departmental structure.

From what is known of TVEI post-sixteen, it has proved to be different in many respects from TVEI pre-sixteen. Much of this appears to be connected with the nature, scale and priorities of the post-sixteen sector. There are numerous areas of concern for those looking for the initiative to have a major impact on post-sixteen education. Many of the implications that can be drawn from comments above reinforce much of what is said in the recommendations made by FEU (*Supporting TVEI*, 1985). The need for a planned, coherent progression within TVEI is of paramount importance for any scheme. Adequate curriculum, staff and institutional development must be embarked upon and the breaking down of school/F.E. barriers and the strengthening of links and liaison should be a priority. The unique nature of F.E. in the educational system and the inherent differences between school and college must be appreciated, planned for at all levels and afforded status, in order to achieve the desired smooth transition and coherence of provision expected within TVEI. Unless these things are implemented in the neglected territory of 16–18 TVEI the four-year programme is in grave danger of becoming a two-plus-two divided initiative, with this second phase offering little coherence and progression other than a narrow banding with YTS, CPVE and related pre-vocational courses.

TVEI is not simply a number of interesting pilot schemes. It constitutes a major initiative to change the education and training of 14–18 year olds and a move towards a more vocationally relevant system. At policy level, TVEI represents an impetus in restructuring the education and training experiences of 14–18 year olds and reorganizing the environment in which they learn. It is claimed to be a catalyst for change by some and divisive by others. Within it, however, there is certainly potential for curriculum change, changes in teaching styles and for a better deal for many young people in schools and colleges (Gleeson and Smith, 1987). Yet in many ways TVEI six years on has not fulfilled its potential – particularly in relation to equal opportunities, teaching styles, cross-curricular development and progression. In the absence of any major policy initiatives in this direction the likelihood remains that TVEI, alongside other pre-vocational and training developments, will constitute a distinct stream for average and low attaining pupils (Blackman, 1987). This does not bode well for an initiative proclaiming to promote flexibility and challenge arbitrary divisions between theoretical and applied knowledge in the curriculum. If TVEI is to avoid becoming a 'sink' subject for the 'less able' more thought and resources will need to be given to progression across the 14–18 age and ability range. What has emerged from the TVEI pilot schemes to date is an authentic response from many teachers and students, leading to a broadening of the curriculum and involving more student-centred, activity-based learning, with new methods of assessment. If such initial motivation is not to be lost some of the more divisive features associated with TVEI policy and practice referred to in this chapter still need to be addressed. It is to this neglected aspect of vocational education and training, and alternatives to it, that the final chapter which follows is addressed.

Notes

1. Originally conceived as a Pilot Project, TVEI was designed to provide a broad and relevant technical and vocational curriculum for 14–18 year old boys and girls across the ability range. The project commenced life in 14 LEAs in 1983 and now involves 103 Projects in LEAs in England, Wales and Scotland. As Figure 4 indicates, TVEI covers a total of approximately 650 schools and colleges incorporating over 80,000 students.

Figure 4

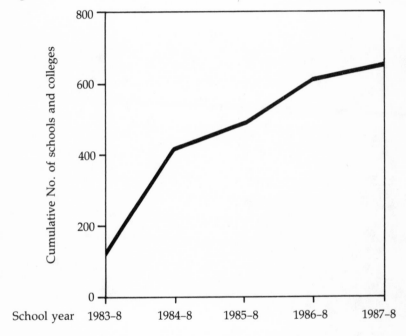

Following on the Government White Paper *Working Together – Education and Training* (1986), TVEI has been extended as a National Scheme to encompass the majority of schools and colleges. Eleven LEAs commenced their Extension programmes in September 1987, with more to follow in September 1988 and thereafter. Something of the importance attached to TVEI is reflected in the funding provided to it: £250m allocated for the pilot period and £900m for its Extension. In addition to providing a relevant and practical preparation for working life, TVEI is committed to a number of key curricular principles, including active learning strategies, cross-curricular developments, school/college progression, equal opportunities, and linking academic and applied areas of the curriculum.

2. I am grateful to Allen Maunders, Gordon Smith and members of the University of Keele Research and Evaluation Unit with whom these and other viewpoints in this chapter have been explored elsewhere, though in different form. See Gleeson, D. and Maunders, A. (1985); Gleeson, D. and Smith, G. (1987). Parts of this paper were originally developed by Gleeson, D. and Smith, G. (1987) and Gleeson, D. (1987).

Training and
Its Alternatives

6

It is perhaps a mistake to view the subject of this chapter, *alternatives*, as just another convenient way of rounding off the discussion. Alternatives are not answers and cannot be readily tacked on at the end. What I have sought to demonstrate in this book is that training is neither a neutral nor an objective process and should not, therefore, be viewed in a political vacuum. This would seem obvious, and yet there are those who see recent training policy as a reformative process[1] when it is in fact a contributory factor to many of the political problems which young people face today. It is to this apparent contradiction between cause and effect that this final chapter is addressed.

So far, I have been critical of an emerging tripartism in further education and training which mainly affects young people in the 16–19 age range. YTS and schemes like it have been criticized for being employer led – often based on sexist and racist divisions – and serving to mitigate the frustration of unemployment justifiably felt by many young adults. Following on such criticisms this chapter argues that the continued influence of the government's New Training Initiative (NTI) on schools and colleges should be reviewed, not least because it reinforces inequalities and arbitrary divisions between education and work. At the moment education and training are currently developing along very separate paths. One group of students experience *education* which is based on the acquisition of knowledge and power, whilst the prevailing pedagogy for those in *training* relies heavily on practical, relevant and vocational skills, separated off from conceptual development (see Young, 1971; Bernstein, 1971; Green, 1986). It is the contention of this chapter that education policy for 16–19 year olds should be one of creating a balanced curriculum which integrates theoretical and practical skills, and which seeks to break down arbitrary divisions between students and trainees and between teachers and trainers. There is, of course, a strongly held belief that the MSC, or Training Commission as it is now called, has done more to improve the opportunities of working class youth than many schools, colleges or LEAs have ever done (Benson and Lansley, 1987). However, as the various research studies looked at so far indicate, this belief is not shared by working class youth themselves, many of whom view YTS and pre-vocational courses with some scepticism and instrumentalism. If, for some, YTS has become the only way into employment, there is little evidence that the *content* of YTS courses is the main contributing factor. Employment is, of course, crucially related to education but there is more to education than specific job prospects on the horizon allow. That such a reality should dictate the content of the 'new' vocational curriculum is, however, paradoxical, not least because it draws attention to the weaknesses of current training policy – namely that it is not actually linked with productive labour or employment.

A better future?

Despite the apparent 'crisis' generated by youth unemployment the promise of a better future via training remains a powerful, if not convenient, ideological form of expression. Yet, as I have sought to argue, when young people are denied entry to the labour market by being made into 'trainees', that does not necessarily mean that they have achieved a greater degree of autonomy or control over their lives. Increased levels of participation in Further Education and training, in other words, cannot simply be equated with expanded opportunity. A principal argument so far has been that mass 'training', in its present form, does little more than institutionalize youth unemployment as an inevitable consequence of the 'market mechanism', and reinforce the generally accepted view that youth employment is a thing of the past.[2] Current training policy, for example, is modelled on the structural inevitability of youth unemployment and this has become a powerful mechanism for stifling social criticism, the consequences of which have not yet been fully realized in conventional political and educational circles. Yet within existing youth training schemes young people are being 'employed' on low wages (adult's work on youth's allowances) often without minimal legal, welfare or trade union protection. If this process is to be challenged then an effective employment and training policy needs to be pursued: one that, for example, establishes work and training as a right for all, in the same manner that legal rights and rights to education, health care, welfare and so forth have become an integral part of the liberal democratic state but which are now under threat (Rustin, 1983). Thus, to view training policy in a vacuum or reformist light without reference to the ways in which it actually generates poverty, unemployment, depresses adult and youth wage levels and limits trade union effectiveness, ignores the political 'function' of training at the present time.

Recent evidence indicates, for example, that training without work may create an underclass that sees itself as not having a stake in mainstream affluent society (Finn, 1987). Already the signs of high levels of political alienation and disillusionment are evident among young people. Reporting on the findings of six studies of young people as part of a major ESRC initiative, McGurk (1987) reports the increasing levels of political illiteracy and racism among young people which his report sees as directly linked with unemployment.

> The overwhelming majority of British Youth appears to be politically illiterate. They have no conception of the structure of society, of how the economy works, of the characteristics of different political systems; and they are hardly aware of the policy issues, let alone the philosophical differences, which distinguish the principal political parties.

Such observations of political illiteracy among British youth are not new, and follow closely on the heels of past interventions, such as the Programme for Political Education initiated by Sir Keith Joseph in the 1970s, and designed to promote political literacy among young people in schools and colleges. However, since the introduction of the New Training Initiative (NTI) in 1981, vocational realism has replaced political idealism, thereby offsetting any critical potential that political education in the curriculum may have realized. Whatever the reality about such critical potential there is little doubt that the New Right has taken political education in the curriculum seriously, not least in their recent representations to Parliament criticizing left-wing and anti-business bias among teachers. Again, despite any lack of evidence from HMI to substantiate such claims the extreme right, in the form of the so-called Hillgate Group, has continued to find favour with the Conservative government and the MSC in effectively censoring political education in many schools and colleges. In the past decade it is perhaps not surprising then that 'new' right views on a range of subjects, including sex, gender and race education, should also find expression and favour with a growing sector of right-wing youth. Evidence drawn from McGurk's ESRC report (1987) indicates that in 1979 just under 7% of those young people interviewed supported the National Front or the British Movement. In 1983 this figure had risen to 14%. If second party preferences are included more than 30% of youngsters expressed some sympathy for a party of the extreme right (Midgley, 1987). Whether or not lack of political education is the 'cause' of this change in attitudes is debatable. However, what is clear is that recent restrictions on what political and other matters teachers can and cannot teach is likely to have far-reaching consequences on the general level of education among young people in the longer term.[3]

Thus, in raising the question about what gets left out of the curriculum (in terms of political education), the issue about what to *include* in the curriculum is also of crucial importance. To date this issue has remained taboo in the sociology of education and among sections of the left, not least because such curricular intervention has been viewed as ideologically suspect or irrelevant. One consequence of this has been that issues regarding the content and control of education have been separated off, reflecting one critic's observation that '. . . it is easier to critique developments in theoretical terms than to contribute more positively to political struggles over the curriculum' (Whitty, 1982; 1985). While the framework of training is at present determined by government policy, it should be recognized that it is largely the institutional process of education itself which is currently legitimating the new training enterprise. Yet, to date, there has been little attempt to challenge recent training initiatives from *within* education and as a consequence the MSC's managing interest has gone largely unopposed. While this partly reflects the weakness of the teaching profession, the unions and the labour movement at the present time, it also represents a deeper cultural ambivalence about the educational requirements of so-called 'less able' young people so far described on a range of pre-vocational and training courses. Perhaps not surprisingly it has been left to this group themselves to indicate their own opposition to the new vocationalism, and what it is that they want from training and work. In this respect it is principally the failure of youth training schemes to become more closely linked with productive labour that is leading trainees and their parents to opt out or vote with their feet. At one level such opposition is expressed in conformist and apathetic ways, to the numbingly unimaginative content of the curriculum, which follows well established lines, such as woodwork, metalwork, painting, decorating, sewing, and so forth (Atkinson, 1983), while, at another, some trainees have organized against YTS schemes, joining unions, 'truanting' and even going on strike. In the 'right to work' marches in the early 1980s, one of the more interesting slogans was 'Jobs not YOPS', to be followed by strikes against YTS in the mid-1980s. It is perhaps important to recognize that such opposition is not principally directed against training as such, but its poor quality and lack of connection with work, career and an income. In these circumstances, withdrawal of social security benefits for those who refuse to undertake such training is little more than State coercion of the most autocratic kind.

It could be argued that the issue of youth unemployment is simply political and economic in nature, the 'solution' to which cannot be conceived in terms of a more enlightened education and training system alone. Having said this, however, the discussion of possible alternatives does not automatically follow. It is also the case, for example, that alienation, racism, lack of opportunities and so forth cannot be explained in terms of the truism 'there ain't no jobs', crucial as this may be. One of the paradoxes of MSC policy is that it has drawn attention to long-standing issues in the relationship between school and work, which predate the rapid increase in unemployment in the late 1970s. Prior to this time little sociological interest was taken in the fate of young workers entering dead-end jobs, the majority of whom had little or no access to further education or training. If the research literature and official documents in this period focused on topics such as 'the transition from school to work', 'occupational choice' and 'career opportunities', the reality open to many young people was that of low paid and unskilled work. Thus, simply to demand a return to the full employment conditions of the 1960s, even if that were possible, ignores the limiting effects of various types of work on young people's long-term social and economic opportunities. As Roberts (1984) has argued, popular as a mass extension of unskilled or semi-skilled work might appear at the present time, it would not alleviate the problem of low pay, boredom and chronic job changing; neither would it clarify what the relationship should be between education, training and work. The problem at the moment is, as I have argued so far, that chronic job changing has been replaced by chronic scheme changing (Raffe, 1983b) without any fundamental appraisal being made of the nature of work itself.

According to Tipton (1983), there is a basic contradiction in much of the current thinking about how to improve the quality of training; its terms are that no questions are being asked about the quality of work, its structure, design, organization and distribution. At present extending training for existing forms of monotonous and humdrum work is likely only to increase conflict and tension between trainees, teachers and employers as expectations are frustrated. To date the nature of work has been taken as given by educationists and others and, as a consequence, few attempts exist to combine policies for training with policies for work design. There is, for example, much talk of the importance of 'labour flexibility' but what does this mean? Findings drawn from industrial relations research indicate little evidence across the economy of any strategic planning by industry incorporating work reorganization or job redesign programmes (Rose and Jones, 1985). Where such programmes do appear they tend to be *ad hoc* involving job rotation, job enlargement, job enrichment, quality circles and 'autonomous work groups'. A principal feature of such initiatives is that they are designed to humanize the work place, while at the same time increasing productivity and managerial control. Yet, if the debate about improving the quality of vocational education in schools and colleges is to be taken seriously, changes in the structure of work must be addressed. It makes little sense, for example, to encourage young people in the skills of working co-operatively, learning by 'doing' and acquiring 'transferable skills,' if employers simply want them to do as they are told. The paradox of training is that teachers, pupils and parents now recognize that this is not simply an education or even an unemployment problem – but a problem about *work itself*. At the moment, however, there is little sign that Conservative Training Policy is doing more than to encourage employer-led definitions of work and training. Supported by the reform of police powers, industrial relations and social security legislation, the government has considerably strengthened management's right to manage. In so doing, discipline and control of the workforce has replaced any serious rethinking on work redesign, worker participation and industrial democracy, all factors which have reverberated back on the national vocational education and training debate. Inevitably in such circumstances training reflects this preoccupation with discipline and control: young people are there to be *trained* independently of whether the jobs are there or not.

On the surface this would seem to add up to bad business, not least because the £3b plus spent by the MSC each year on training contributes little directly to productivity and profits.[4] However, as I have sought to argue, Conservative Training Policy is not concerned primarily with short-term profits, but rather with the long-term restructuring of working class attitudes and relations to work among the population. It is this political dimension of training which requires critical attention, not least because it equates profit and productivity with employer-led control, to the exclusion of all other forms of democratic participation. Yet, in practice, there is no inalienable reason why education, training and work should be employer led, narrow and prescriptive. Production and productivity are not just about profit and the subordination of labour to management control, they are also connected with *human* production and productivity. In other words, human endeavour and expression involves more than the relationship of discrete individuals to jobs which the detailed construction of tasks allows (Knights *et al.*, 1985). Moreover, evidence indicates that on a wide range of issues employers do not know what they want, perhaps a further indication of the danger of opting for a predominantly employer-led vision of the world (Gleeson and Mardle, 1980).

Yet, as Tipton (1983) rightly argues, training *is* for jobs. The likelihood is that little will be achieved on this front until a legal duty is placed on employers to consult with unions on all training issues, and the right to education and training is placed on the collective bargaining agenda. Despite the obvious pitfalls, only the redefining and restructuring of work patterns can offer the possibility that 'training for work' may take on a broader meaning than the present narrow vocationalism allows. Little will happen on this front until trade unions are more actively involved in industrial democracy (Bullock, 1977) and government and industry legally obliged to co-operate in matters regarding work design, training and the continuing further education of *all* workers. Without such co-operation it is unlikely that training provision in its present form will inspire much confidence or public support.

If, in the short term, jobs are not available to 16–19 year olds they should not be fobbed off with 'cottage industry' employment (handyman repairs, gardening, delivering, housework, helping the aged and so forth) or compensated for their loss with remedial schemes that do little more than infantilize them and make them even more dependent on the state and their parents. It is this aspect rather than unemployment itself that perhaps constitutes the present 'crisis', and poses as much a political as an economic problem. The obvious need at present is to consider programmes for education and training alongside a programme for jobs. Education and training without the possibility of employment as a foreseeable goal is not only politically unacceptable but also likely to cast doubt, no matter what the quality, on the various types of training provided (Roberts, 1984). What is required now are policies that do not simply delay entry into work or provide employers with cheap labour (this only exacerbates unemployment) but offer young people systematic career develop- ment, training and opportunities for full-time skilled work (Casson, 1979).

While any proposal to extend employment opportunities may prove unpopular with Thatcherite politicians and monetarists (such as the ILEA's 'job guarantee' scheme),[5] mainly because it acknowledges the failure of the market to redistribute resources, historical circumstances (notably in the post-war period) suggest that full employment is by no means an impossible dream, even in times of economic recession. Moreover, the high cost of unemployment subsidies, benefits, tax and national insurance loss, and of rent and rate income, suggests there is little economic reason to doubt why a policy of full employment should not be actively pursued at the present time. Furthermore, there is no reason why training provision, linked to a policy of full employment, should follow existing institutional arrangements or be completed in some predefined way by the age of eighteen or twenty. Greater flexibility and choice by youth and adults about where and when they undertake training, and at what level and at what point in their lives, would certainly focus more critical attention on the least examined aspect of the present debate about training, namely, the use and relevance of training to young people themselves.

It might, of course, be argued that the pursuit of such an alternative viewpoint in Britain at the moment is unrealistic: that Conservative rhetoric about consumer choice does not allow for young people or workers to make decisions about their own working lives. But, as I have sought to argue in this book, existing training initiatives are equally unrealistic: 'training for the dole' (Cohen, 1982; Finn, 1987) being perhaps the most naive form of idealism yet invented. It is only by starting to debate such matters that the present arrangements of training may be challenged. However, any programme for change cannot consist of a purely 'conceptual alternative' (Hoare, 1967); it also involves integrating theoretical and practical issues which take account of the young workers' *active participation* in the work and training process. In this respect a number of important policy recommendations have been recently advocated, including:

- the establishment of rights for trainees and students to negotiate their own education and training and to enjoy equality of choice;
- legislation to require employers to release employees for education – first as youth, and later, as adults;
- . . . two years of education and training on a voluntary basis for all . . . the provision of 'through routes' to further study on all existing courses, as part of the redesign of 16–19 curriculum and assessment;
- all training to be in real skills leading to nationally recognized qualifications;
- all training to lead to real jobs in socially useful work.[6]

Such recommendations not only involve teachers, educationists, trade unions and others in contesting the unfamiliar terrain of vocational education, they also involve considering training schemes which negate the vital interests of young people and which emasculate them. However, these recommendations are likely to pale into insignificance if both an educational policy and an enlightened funding programme for 16–19 year olds are not found to address the present patchwork nature of non-advanced F.E. provision. At the root of the problem is a totally inadequate system of financial provision for students in this age group; at the moment their lack of political muscle renders them prey to parental dependence, discretionary grants or the MSC's 'shilling'. While the situation of such students is unlikely to stir so much as a back-bench revolt, the sheer size of the problem suggests that jerry-built training will, in the long term, not succeed.

Yet, given that increasing numbers of school leavers are unlikely to enter the labour market much before 18 or 19, the arguments for building a comprehensive education and training system are compelling. However, such a system must not be designed merely to delay entry into work or replicate what has already gone on in school. What is called for is a system of *education* and *training* which equally focuses on student needs and requirements both within and outside the labour market. Regional, demographic, occupational and other factors have not only altered the structural relationship between school and work, they have also called into question present makeshift arrangements for regulating young people's entry to the labour market. To date there has been no concerted attempt to develop a co-ordinated education and training policy for the 16–19 age group as a whole. Instead, we have witnessed a succession of right-wing critiques of standards in education and the assumed failure of teachers to direct pupils towards more vocationally relevant subjects. Meanwhile, the traditional examination system has remained untouched other than in terms of tinkering with the GCE/CSE (GCSE) system and introducing a confusing array of 16 and 17+ pre-vocational reforms. As such the 'new' vocationalism has, under the direction of MSC and NCVQ, followed a separate path from mainstream schooling and has done little to challenge entrenched assumptions regarding high status knowledge in the curriculum and its close association with the examination system and the labour market hierarchy. In this respect, the dominant emphasis on theoretical, abstract and scientific knowledge has gone largely unquestioned by the MSC. For the so-called disadvantaged, however, the dominant pedagogic experience has been extended and remains firmly anchored within practical, relevant and vocational knowledge; a form of control traditionally associated with ensuring the lower orders' obligation to the system and their awareness of its dominant moral codes (Meyer, 1977; Atkinson, 1983).[7] In this respect investment in 'voc prep' fulfils a hitherto ignored class and reproduction function – that of safeguarding traditional academic knowledge by preventing its proliferation to the masses whose participation in extended education ('access' and staying on) might otherwise dilute the vocational relevance of academic qualifications to the middle class (Johnson, 1982). If this might, on the surface, seem far fetched it has to be viewed alongside the New Right's paranoia about the dilution of academic standards, seen to be associated with the growth of comprehensive education, active learning and developments such as GCSE, A/S levels and other 'progressive' reforms.

Thus, it is within this broader context that training not only separates off various categories of young people as distinct social and intellectual types and on criteria which have only marginal relevance to the kinds of jobs they are likely to perform, but it also becomes indistinguishable from the labour market that it once 'served'. At the moment, we are training young people in this country by default mainly because they did not achieve academically at school, which inevitably downgrades their experience of vocational education and training. For many, F.E. and training represents little more than an administrative device for excluding them from the labour market, thereby deferring the 'problem of the transition from school to work' to 18, 19 and beyond. Coupled with this, poor rates of pay and threats of cuts in benefits for those who refuse training reinforce the view among many that F.E. and training represents simply a form of compulsory cheap labour. Yet it makes little sense to bureacratically debar all young people from entering work at 16 simply to pump up acceptable staying-on rates. This not only makes a nonsense of the term 'progression' but it can also adversely influence the employment opportunities of some young people seeking jobs at 16.

Going tertiary?

Perhaps the least considered aspect of the 1988 Education Act is where 16–19 policy fits into the changing arrangements of post-16 progression. This is the one age group neglected in the Act, yet it is the stage most urgently in need of a coherent new approach (*TES* Editorial, 4.12.87). At the moment provision is disparate and *ad hoc*: sixth forms and sixth form colleges, F.E. and tertiary colleges are often in competition with one another for declining numbers of 16–19 year olds. Moreover, the introduction of City Technology Colleges, selection and the threat of 'opting out' have intensified such competition, rendering the range of courses and options on offer in some institutions severely restricted. Perhaps not surprisingly, and in the absence of a positive lead at local and national level, much duplication exists between the competing strands of post-16 provision.

Part of this debate, reflected in the correspondence pages of the *TES* (Autumn 1987) focuses upon the relative merits of tertiary and sixth form colleges over traditional further education and schooling to offer a genuinely comprehensive system of provision. According to Galloway (1987) this debate is observable in new tertiary colleges which draw their staff from both the school and the F.E. sectors. Mutual suspicion often initially prevails fuelled by the sense that the new institution is making too many concessions to the ethos of the other. Fears among staff drawn from F.E. often refer to the dominance of 'A' levels and F.E. traditions being submerged, with academic courses thriving at the expense of vocational and non-vocational work. In other respects, school staff often mistrust the entrepreneurial style of F.E. teachers who, in their attitudes towards teaching, are seen to be didactic and instrumental.

Clearly such views reflect deeper and more fundamental divisions in post-16 education than have been given credit for here. However, in the present climate they are likely to set tertiary college against F.E. and school against college, in a debate that is in danger of losing sight of the students. At the moment going tertiary has been presented in some quarters as a panacea for all the ills associated with traditional post-16 provision, but with little attention paid to the comprehensive educational processes involved. However, the issue is not what one should call 16–19 provision, F.E. or tertiary, but what its *practice* should be for all 16–19 year olds across the present tripartite divide, irrespective of class, race and gender. If tertiary education is to be more than a pot-pourri of the competing facets of post-16 provision, it will need to heed the historical lessons of comprehensive education, not least in challenging the academic, technical and vocational divisions which arbitrarily separate off young people in classrooms and in the work place (Hargeaves, 1982; Reynolds *et al.*, 1987).

In reality, not all students want to stay on after 16, enter skilled training or pursue a career immediately on leaving school, although they may wish to do so later. The real need is to flexibly integrate work training and education on more comprehensive lines, fostering notions of continuing education, involving rights of access, which take into account young people's varying abilities, interests and ambitions over time. What young people need to escape from is the depressing scenario of dependency, of being bounced from one training scheme to another under the watchful eye of government agencies such as MSC, DHSS and so forth. While such scrutiny may improve the overall level of student participation rates in F.E. and training, the gains are likely to be short lived and the longer term returns seen by students to be of little value.

Whatever happened to general education?

As noted in the previous chapter, perhaps the major weakness of contemporary training policy is that it neither specifies skills training nor provides an adequate general education. Thus, under present conditions, the young lose out both ways; on the one hand, they do not gain marketable or recognized skills and, on the other, they do not acquire knowledge and understanding, however broadly defined, that allows them critical insight into the political or economic workings of society. Perhaps, not surprisingly, the expansion of vocational training has resulted in inferior general education, without the employment prospects of young people altering much one way or the other. One effect of YTS, and also TVEI, is that they can force young people to settle on vocational training and employment options too early on, in many cases prior to the fourth year at school. Despite the publicity given to core curriculum and transferable skills training, early specialization narrows the options open to young people later on in life. Consequently, without a broadly based general education it is most unlikely that students will be able to utilize forms of training that they have not been educated to absorb. The danger is that youth in Britain is fast becoming over trained and under educated, at a time when the general education base of most other industrial nations is broadening rather than narrowing around 'skills' training.

There is at the present time in Britain an obsession with the terms 'skill' and 'skill ownership'. It has come to represent the practical application of almost all facets of human performance and everyday life not encapsulated in mainstream subjects or time-served training. Syllabuses and course outlines, for example, repeatedly emphasize the importance of students achieving *skill ownership*, which they may apply in a variety of occupational and social settings. Hence, enterprise skills, skills for living, transferable skills, interpersonal skills and so forth, are all given a high profile in the behavioural objectives which support pre-vocational and training schemes. Such 'skills' are premised on the assumed lack of relevance of the mainstream curriculum which, critics argue, emphasizes theoretical understanding at the expense of practical application. While there may be some truth in this, there is little evidence that the skills-based approach being put forward plugs the skill gap. If anything, it has become tacked on rather than integrated within the mainstream curriculum, reinforcing existing distinctions between knowledge, experience and understanding. As Wellington (1987) has argued, 'skills' are not entities in themselves, separated off from the people in whom they reside:

> Skills do not exist in their own right. Employers do not recruit skills. They recruit people. Skills reside in people and are acquired by people.
>
> Skills are not entities which are in short supply. What industries need are people with the abilities to develop new skills, to learn new knowledge, to acquire new concepts and theories and to adapt to technological change with enthusiasm and lack of fear. This is the essential meaning of technological literacy as opposed to technological skill . . . The job of both education and training is surely to provide people with the ability and enthusiasm to learn, to adapt to change, and to be aware of and at home with new technology.
>
> In addition, the development of critical and creative abilities (not skills) would seem to be a necessity for innovation. The aims of education should be couched in these terms, rather than in exhausted and overstretched language of skills which is barking up the wrong linguistic tree. Companies don't recruit or employ skills – they employ people.

All the indications are that employers, educationists and others do not recognize the relevance of contemporary 'skills training', which is not seen to embody the general indicators of competence required to gain access to the job market (Holt, 1987). It is perhaps time to recognize that experimentation with generic skills training has been a failure, and that the sacrifice of general education for a gain in vocationalism has not been worth the trade (Jackson, 1981). The perfunctory time accorded to either learning technical 'know-how' or acquiring general knowledge suggests that students are getting neither education nor training. The irony, as Willis (1984) has pointed out, is that working-class youth who know much about work, and are prepared to put up with its most boring and exploited forms, should have basic work skills pushed down their throats from a very early age. Moreover, the fact that so few workers eventually end up in trades for which they were trained suggests that training without general education has, anyway, little vocational relevance. The likelihood is that a broadly-based education, which combines learning about work alongside the study of society, including options drawn from the arts, sciences, humanities, social sciences and community, will in the long run have more public support and perhaps possess greater vocational relevance. At the moment, the greatest weakness of the new vocationalism is its failure to capture the enthusiasm and inspire the imagination of young people. Its dull utilitarianism and endless messages about the virtues of enterprise and entrepreneurialism reinforce the suspicious isolation in which young people are viewed in society. Essentially, the message of the new vocationalism is that young people cannot be trusted to identify with, or learn the skills necessary to reproduce, contemporary 'enterprise culture'. Almost to reinforce this message those areas of knowledge associated with art, music, literature, political education and popular culture, which might turn the heads of young people, have been edited out of the new vocationalism in favour of an overtly *materialist* curriculum. According to Pring (1987):

> There, indeed, lies the most serious criticism of the new vocationalism for, where it fudges the distinctions between 'training' and 'education', or fastens on to the model of 'skills training', or maintains the erroneous separation of work from pleasure, or comprehends educational aims in terms of utility, the key educational (and vocational) task of developing youngsters as persons become submerged and the arts become an embarrassment – something for the less serious, leisure moments of one's life. But, to the contrary, the arts and the humanities should be central to education – to the development of that reflective state of mind in which one comes to understand what it is to be and to grow as 'a person' in all its facets, and vocational education should respect that preparation. Not to so respect entails a curtailment of growth, a narrowing of vision, an impoverishment of emotional life, and a barrier to critical judgement, which may provide a vocational *training* for some aspects of industry, but hardly the vocational *education* that a healthy and democratically run society would require. And, indeed, it is a major task for the arts and humanities to re-examine their place in the new circumstances, and to explore the curriculum implications of giving the arts a central role in a more vocationally oriented education. Certainly, 'arts for leisure' won't do, because the artist is a serious person, not a playboy, and through the arts and humanities the values, which determine our notions of 'vocationalism', would be explored in all seriousness.

This is not to advocate piecemeal injections of art, liberal studies or political education, which in the 1960s and 1970s, were driven like a wedge into the vocational curriculum to offset the worst effects of over-specialization and alienation. What is called for at the present time is a curriculum that integrates arts, sciences, social sciences and humanities with practical vocational skills, and which seeks to break down existing tripartite divisions. Bringing education back in will not be an easy task, not least because the terms and conditions of conventional liberal humanist education have changed. As Tipton (1983) has argued previously, if educationists and teachers feel understandably squeamish about becoming involved in 'narrow' training, then the solution is to reconstitute the debate surrounding the relationship between education, training and work. Perhaps the major starting point here is to define vocational education and training more broadly, to emphasize youth's active involvement in, rather than separation from, mainstream society. As one commentator has noted, it is not dole, schools or work experience that the young unemployed require now but 'schools and' (in a well-known phrase) 'really useful education and rewarding, unexploitative work' (Horne, 1983).

Part of the argument of this book has been that the 'alternatives' so far considered cannot be viewed in isolation. They involve a radically different way of making sense of the relations between education, training and work, and represent a rejection of the political assumptions about human nature that inform Conservative Training Policy. Instead, the active role of the student learning within and outside the workplace is stressed, accentuating the social and political processes involved in linking vocational education and training with productive labour. At the moment the lack of relationship between training and productive labour has led to policies based on the *containment* of youth, involving discipline, manipulation and employer-led considerations above all else. In the absence of work government training policy has been aggressively marketed as the only available alternative open to young people. Yet, as we have seen, many young people reject training without work on the grounds that it is second rate and second best, while others accept it because they have little other choice.

At the present time vocational education and training provision for the majority of school leavers remains patchy and meets the needs of neither individual nor society. In recession government and employers have abandoned any long-term education and training plans, preferring to regulate youth unemployment via special measures and categorical funding. In the circumstances, the folly of allowing employers to dictate training policy will undoubtedly have far-reaching effects, not least in reducing skill levels and educational standards throughout the work force. Ultimately, responsibility for this rests with government, employers and the MSC who have failed to establish a coherent policy of education, training and work, and who have sought to control rather than mobilize the labour force via vocational training. In this respect the MSC has done little to extend or to improve the quality of further education or training, and has reinforced inequalities by experimenting with 'skills' training, with little regard for the education of the whole person.

Yet, despite this apparently depressing scenario, there remains some room for manoeuvre in implementing change at the local level. As we have seen, the paradox of training reflects the simultaneous emergence of two potentially conflicting developments (Harland, 1987). On the one hand, it reflects strong central control of a kind which has permitted the detailed intervention of government and employer influence right down to the classroom level. On the other, YTS, TVEI and a variety of other pre-vocational courses support local initiatives which, in many cases, are highly experimental and creative. Thus, if at one level the ratchet of central control has tightened, at another, the local level, 'progressive' approaches associated with active learning and equal opportunities, integrated approaches, cross-curricular development and so forth, have forced a rethink about the processes through which young people are educated and trained (Pring, 1985a). If, in the short term, much of what passes for vocational education and training leaves much to be desired, at least the issues involved are now openly on the agenda. No longer can it be said that further education and training is a backwater of the education system with relevance for only a minority of school leavers. By placing vocational education and training initiatives at the centre of the stage government policy has drawn public attention to hitherto ignored issues, in particular, the failure of government training policy itself. For this reason alone it is unlikely that the debate regarding the future direction of further education and training will remain the same. Moreover, there is, as McCulloch (1987) has argued, nothing intrinsically narrow, right-wing or conservative about technical and vocational knowledge – it remains very much what society makes of it. Historically, the debate about the aims of vocational education and training is recurring (Reeder, 1981), and reflects wider social and political arguments over the nature of British Society itself. Thus, despite the divisions and distinctions made apparent by training policy, it is equally important to recognize that, in quite unintended ways, there is now greater awareness of what should be on the education and training agenda and what is worth pursuing. It is as a contribution to the neglected aspect of this 'recurring debate' that this book is addressed.

Notes:

1. See Benson and Lansley (1987), *op. cit.*
2. Or, conversely, that youth *unemployment* in the 16–18 age range is a thing of the past, i.e. training as a substitute for employment.
3. See, for example, the 'celebrated' Clause 28. Although also see the Education Act (1986).
4. For a detailed statistical breakdown of these figures, see Note 1, Chapter 1, pages 15–17
5. Though of course ILEA's 'job guarantee' scheme (in conjunction with the London Enterprise Agency), represented an innovative step forward in securing school leavers employment. However, in breaking up ILEA the Conservative government has, under its inner city 'schools/industry compact' scheme, taken over ILEA's initiative but without giving ILEA any credit for it. According to the *TES* (11.3.88) '. . . there is something unbelievably childish in this desire to slight the ILEA: certainly it does nothing to foster a belief that Ministers understand or care about the close co-operation between education authorities and industry which is needed if the ''compact'' idea is to spread' (p. 2).
6. Adapted from 'The Youth Training Scheme: A Strategy for the Labour Movement'. *Socialist Society* (1983).
7. See Young, M.F.D. (Ed) (1971): *Knowledge and Control*. Collier Macmillan.

Glossary of Terms

ATP	Adult Employment Training Programme (see 'ET')
BERA	British Educational Research Association
B/TEC	Business and Technician Education Council
CEE	Certificate of Extended Education
CCETSW	Central Council for the Education and Training of Social Work
CD	Curriculum Development
CDT	Craft, Design and Technology
CEO	Chief Education Officer
CGLI	City and Guilds of London Institute
CPVE	Certificate of Pre-Vocational Education
CSE	Certificate of Secondary Education
CTC	City Technology College
DES	Department of Education and Science
DOE	Department of Employment
DTI	Department of Trade and Industry
EITB	Engineering Industry Training Board
EOC	Equal Opportunities Commission
ESG	Education Support Grant
ET	Employment Training Programme
F.E.	Further Education
FEU	Further Education Unit
GCE	General Certificate of Education
GERBIL	Great Education Reform Bill
GCSE	General Certificate of Secondary Education
GRIST	Grant Related In-Service Training
HE	Higher Education
HMI	Her Majesty's Inspector (or Inspectorate)

ILEA	Inner London Education Authority
IMS	Institute of Manpower Studies
INSET	In-Service Education for Teachers
IS	Integrated Science
IT	Information Technology
LAPP	Low Attaining Pupil Project
LEA	Local Education Authority
MSC	Manpower Services Commission (now The Training Commission)
NAFE	Non-Advanced Further Education
NATFHE	National Association of Teachers in Further and Higher Education
NCVQ	National Council for Vocational Qualifications
NFER	National Foundation for Educational Research
NTI	New Training Initiative
NUS	National Union of Students
NVQ	National Vocational Qualifications
OTFs	Occupational Training Families
PICKUP	Professional, Industrial and Commercial Updating
PS	Problem Solving
PSD	Personal and Social Development
PTRs	Pupil/Teacher Ratios
PVE	Pre-Vocational Education
RAC	Regional Advisory Council
RCB	Regional Curriculum Base
RSA	Royal Society of Arts
RVQ	Review of Vocational Qualifications
SCDC	Schools Curriculum Development Committee
SIP	Schools Industry Project
SLS	Social and Life Skills
SMA	Science Masters Association
TA	Training Agency
TC	Training Commission
TOPS	Training Opportunities Scheme
TUC	Trades Union Congress
TRIST	TVEI Related In-Service Training
TSAS	Training Standards and Advisory Service
TVEI	Technical and Vocational Education Initiative
UVP	Unified Vocational Preparation
WEP	Work Experience Programme
WRNAFE	Work-Related Non-Advanced Further Education
YOP	Youth Opportunities Scheme
YTS	Youth Training Scheme

Bibliography

Ainley, P. (1985) 'More carrots for the school room dafties.' *New Statesman*, 5 July.

Anderson, D. (1982) 'Educated for unemployment.' *Agenda for Debate No. 2*. The Social Affairs Unit.

Atkins, M.J. (1987) 'The pre-vocational curriculum: a review of the issues involved.' *Journal of Curriculum Studies*, Vol. 19. No. 1.

Atkinson, P. (1983) 'Industrial training for the disadvantaged.' *In* Gleeson, D. (1983) *Youth Training and the Search for Work*. London, Routledge and Kegan Paul.

Atkinson, P., Dickinson, H. and Erben, M. (1986) 'The classification and control of vocational training for young people.' *In* Walker, S. and Barton, L. (Eds) (1986) *Youth Unemployment and Schooling*. Milton Keynes, Open University Press.

Atkinson, P. and Rees, T. (1982) *Youth Unemployment and State Intervention*. London, Routledge and Kegan Paul.

Audit Commission (1985) *Obtaining Better Value from FE*. London, HMSO.

Avis, J. (1981) 'Social and technical relations: the case of further education.' *B.J.Soc.of Ed.'* 2(2).

B/TEC (1984) *Policies and Priorities in the 1990s*. London, B/TEC.

Barnes, D. (1987) 'A first impression: TVEI in six schools.' *In* Gleeson, D. (Ed) (1987) *TVEI and Secondary Education: A Critical Appraisal*. Milton Keynes, Open University Press.

Barton, L. and Walker, S. (1986) (Eds) *Youth Unemployment and Schooling*. Milton Keynes, Open University Press.

Bates, I., Clarke J., Cohen, P., Finn, D., Moore, R. and Willis, P. (1984) *Schooling for the Dole*. London, Macmillan.

Benn, C. and Fairley, J. (1986) *Challenging the MSC on Jobs, Education and Training*. London, Pluto Press.

Benson, G. and Lansley, S. (1987) 'Failing the masses, passing the buck.' *New Statesman*, 11 September.

Bernstein, B. (1971) 'On the classification and training of educational knowledge.' *In* Young, M.F.D. (1971) *Knowledge and Control*. Basingstoke, Collier Macmillan.

Blackman, S. (1987) 'The labour market in school: new vocationalism and issues of socially ascribed discrimination.' *In* Brown, P. and Ashton D.N. (1987) *Education, Unemployment and Labour Markets*. New York, Falmer Press.

Blunden, G. (1983) 'Typing in the Tech: domesticity, ideology and women's place in further education.' *In* Gleeson, D. (1983) *op. cit.*

Bowes, A. (1987) *CPVE: A case study of prevocational education*. MA Dissertation. Keele, University of Keele.

Bristow, A.J. (1976) *Inside the College of Further Education*. London, HMSO.

Broady, D. (1981) 'Critique of the economy of education.' *Economy & Industrial Democracy*, Vol. 2. No. 2.

Brown, C. (1984) *Black and White Britain*. London, PSI.

Brown, P. and Ashton, D.N. (1987) *Education, Unemployment and Labour Markets*. New York, Falmer Press.

Burgess, T. (1977) *Education After School*. Harmondsworth, Penguin.

Burgess, T. and Pratt, J. (1974) *Polytechnics: A Report*. London, Pitman.

Callaghan, J. (1976) *Ruskin Speech*. Ruskin College, Oxford, 18 October 1986.

Cantor, L. and Roberts I. (1974) *Further Education Today*. London, Routledge and Kegan Paul. (Revised 1987.)

Casson, M. (1979) *Youth Unemployment*. London, Macmillan.

Chitty, C. (1986) 'TVEI: the MSC's Trojan horse. *In* Benn and Fairley (Eds) (1986) *Challenging the MSC: On Jobs, Education and Training*. London, Pluto Press.

Clough, E., Gray, J. and Jones, B. (1987) 'Those who say no to YTS: findings from the National Youth Cohort Study.' *The British Journal of Education and Work*, Vol. 1. No. 2.

Cockburn, C. (1987) *Two Track Training*. London, Macmillan.

Cohen, P. (1982) 'School for dole.' *New Socialist*, Jan/Feb.

(1986) 'No kidding, it's really useful knowledge.' *Social Science Teacher*.

Collins, R. (1979) *The Credential Society*. New York, Academic Press.

Crowther Report (1959) *'15–18' Central Advisory Council for Education*. London, HMSO.

Dale, R. (1985) *Education, Training and Employment: Towards a New Vocationalism?* Oxford, Pergamon Press.

(1986) (Ed) *Education and Employers' Needs*. Oxford, Oxford University Press/Pergamon Press.

Dancy, J. (Ed) (1984) *TVEI perspectives 14*. Department of Education, Exeter, University of Exeter.

Dennehy, D. (1984) 'Members in YTS: a plea.' *NATFHE Journal*, October.

DES (1984) *Training for Jobs*. White Paper, London, HMSO.

(1985) *Better Schools*. White Paper, London, HMSO.

(1985a) *Education and Training for Young People*. White Paper, London, HMSO.

(1985b) *The Technical and Vocational Education Initiative: Early Developments*. HMI Report, London, HMSO.

(1985c) *Statistical Bulletin 5/85*. London, DES Statistics Branch.

(1985d) *Statistical Bulletin. 9/85*. London, DES Statistics Branch.

(1986a) *Working Together – Education and Training*. White Paper, London, HMSO.

(1986b) *City Technology Colleges. A New Choice of School*. Stanmore, DES.

(1987) *Projected Numbers of Students in Maintained Colleges Studying on Non Advanced Courses: England: 1986–2000*. London, DES Statistics Branch.

(1988) *Training for Employment*. London, HMSO.

Dex, S. (1983) 'Second chances? Further education, ethnic minorities and labour markets.' *In* Gleeson, D. (1983) *op. cit.*

DOE (1981) *A New Training Initiative: A Programme for Action.* London, HMSO.
  (1984) *Training for Jobs.* White Paper London, HMSO.

Durkheim, E. (1977) *The Evolution of Educational Thought.* London, Routledge and Kegan Paul,.

Education Act 1944, London, HMSO.

Eggleston, J. (1977) *The Ecology of the School.* London, Methuen.

Esland, G. and Cathcart, H. (1984) 'The compliant creative worker.' Paper presented at the SSRC/CEDEFOP Conference on the transition between School and Work. Berlin 1984.

Evans, J. and Davies, B. (1986) 'Fixing the mix in TVEI.' Paper presented to the International Sociology of Education Conference, Westhill, Birmingham, January 1986.
  (1987) 'The social context of educational opportunities in new vocational education initiatives.' *In* Gleeson, D. (1987) *op. cit.*

FEU (1979) *A Basis for Choice.* London, FEU.
  (1980) *Developing Social and Life Skills.* London, FEU.
  (1985) *Supporting TVEI.* London, FEU.
  (1986) *CPVE9.* London, FEU.

Fairley, J. and Grahl, J. (1983) 'Conservative training policy and the alternatives.' *Socialist and Economic Review*, Autumn .

Farley, M. (1985) 'Trends and structural changes in English vocational education.' *In* Dale, R. (1985) *op. cit.*

Felton, D. (1987) 'New scheme for long term jobless.' *The Independent*, 19 November.

Fenton, I. *et al.* (1984) *Ethnic Minorities and the YTS.* London, MSC.

Finn, D. (1985) 'The Manpower Services Commission and the Youth Training Scheme; a permanent bridge to work?' *In* Dale, R. (1985) *op. cit.*
  (1987) *Training Without Work: New Deals and Broken Promises.* London, Macmillan.

Fowler, G. (1985) 'What is TVEI?' *Liberal Education*, 54.

Freshwater, M.R. (1982) *Using a Basic Skills Checklist.* Vol. 1. London, MSC.

Galloway, M. (1987) 'Choice but not equality – the tertiary debate.' *Times Educational Supplement*.

Gibb, V. (1983) 'The recreation and perpetuation of the secretarial myth.' *In* Gleeson, D. (1983) *op. cit.*

Gleeson, D. (1980) 'Streaming at work and college.' *Sociological Review*, November.
  (1981) 'Communality and conservatism in teacher education.' *British Journal of Sociology of Education*, Vol. 2. No. 3.
  (1983) *Youth Training and the Search for Work.* London, Routledge and Kegan Paul.
  (1984) 'On the politics of youth training.' *Educational Review*, Birmingham University, Vol. 36 No. 2.
  (1985) 'The privatisation of industry and the nationalisation of youth.' *In* Dale, R. (1985) *op. cit.*
  (1986) 'Life Skills Training and the Politics of Personal Effectiveness.' *Sociological Review* Vol. 34. No. 2.
  (1987) (Ed) *TVEI and Secondary Education: A Critical Appraisal.* Milton Keynes, Open University Press.

Gleeson, D. and Hopkins, M. (1987) 'Further education without tiers.' *Critical Social Policy*, No. 19.

Gleeson, D. and Mardle, G. (1980) *Further Education or Training?* London, Routledge and Kegan Paul.

Gleeson, D. and Maunders, A. (1985) *Curricular Issues in TVEI Evaluation: A Discussion Document.* Keele, University of Keele TVEI Evaluation Unit.

Gleeson, D. and Smith, G. (1987) '16–18: The neglected territory of TVEI provision.' In Gleeson, D. (Ed) (1987) *op. cit.*

Gleeson, D. and Whitty, G. (1976) *Developments in Social Studies Teaching.* Shepton Mallet, Somerset, Open Books.

Golby, G. (1985) 'The coming crisis at 14+.' *Forum*, Vol. 27 No. 3.

Gorbutt, D. (1984) 'The new vocationalism: a critical note.' *In* Dancy, J. (1984) *op. cit.*

Gorringe, R. (1987) *Behaviour and Motivation: Distruption in FE.* London, FEU.

Green, A. (1986) 'The MSC and the three tier structure of FE'. *In* Benn, C and Fairley, J. (1986) *op. cit.*

Hargreaves, D. (1982) *The Challenge for the Comprehensive School.* London, Routledge and Kegan Paul.

Harland, J. (1987) 'The TVEI experience: issues of control, response and the professional role of teachers.' *In* Gleeson, D. (Ed) (1987) *op. cit.*

Harrison, M. (1987) *The TVEI Curriculum 14–16: A Summary.* Leeds, University of Leeds, School of Education. MSC.

Haslegrave Report (1969) *Report of the Committee on Technician courses and Examinations.* London, HMSO.

Hayes, C. (1983) 'Taking your skills with you.' *Times Educational Supplement*, 20 May.

(1983) *Training for Skill Ownership. Learning to take it with you.* Brighton, Institute of Manpower Studies. University of Sussex.

HMI Report (1985) *The Technical and Vocational Education Initiative: Early Developments.* London, HMSO.

HMI Sainsbury Report: 'Grocer caters for own training needs.' *Times Educational Supplement*, 11 September.

Hoare, Q. (1967) 'Education; programmes and men.' *New Left Review*, 32.

Holt, M. (Ed) (1987) *Skills and Vocationalism: The Easy Answer.* Oxford, Oxford University Press.

Hordley, I. and Lee, J. (1970) 'The alternative route: social change and opportunity in technical education.' *Sociology*, 4.

Horne, J. (1983) 'Youth unemployment programmes: a historical account of the development of dole colleges.' *In* Gleeson, D. (1983) *op. cit.*

Horton, C. (1985) 'Nothing like a Job.' *Youthaid*.

Hull (1987) *NAFE in Practice: A HMI Survey.* London, HMSO.

Jackson, P. (1981) *Secondary Schooling for the Poor.* Daedalus Fall.

James, E. (Chairman) (1972) *Teacher Education and Training.* London, HMSO.

Jamieson, I. and Watts. A. (1987) 'Squeezing out enterprise.' *Times Educational Supplement*, 18 December.

Jenkins, R. and Hutson, S. (1986) *Young People, Unemployment and the Family.* Swansea, Swansea School of Social Studies, University College, Swansea.

Johnson, R. (1982) 'Learning for life.' *Schooling and Culture*, 12.

Joint Board (1987) *The Right Pegs in the Right Holes.* London, Joint Board.

Knights, D. *et al.* (1985) *Job Redesign: Cultural Perspective in the Labour Process.* Aldershot, Gower.

Lee, D. (1983) 'Social policy and institutional autonomy in further education.' *In* Gleeson, D. (1983) *op. cit.*

Lee, D., Marsden, D., Hardley, M., Rickman, P. and Manters, K. (1987) 'Youth training: life chances and orientations to work: a case study of the Youth Training Scheme.' *In* Brown, P. and Ashton D.N. (1987) *Education, Unemployment and Labour Markets*. New York, Falmer Press.

Lee, G. and Wrench, J. (1984) '16–18: the crisis of the school leaver.' *Universities Quarterly*, Autumn.

Lempert, W. (1981) 'Perspectives of vocational education in W. Germany and other capitalist countries.' *Economy and Industrial Democracy*, 2.1.

Lenhardt, G. (1981) 'School and wage labour.' *Economy and Industrial Democracy*, 2,1.

Lewis, I. (1986) *TVEI in Theory and Practice: A Comparative Study*. MEd Dissertation. Department of Education, Keele, University of Keele.

Lewis, P. (1987) 'YTS or else.' *New Society*, 28 August.

Liberal Education (1987) 'B/TEC training the core No 57.' Autumn.

Marsland, D. (1987) *Bias Against Business: Anti Capitalist Inclinations in Modern Sociology*. London, The Educational Research Trust.

McCabe, C. (1986) *The Management of Sixteen Plus Choice: in the Organisation of the Early Years of the Technical and Vocational Education Initiative*. (Ed) McCabe, C. Multilingual Matters, Avon.

McCulloch, G. (1987) 'History and policy: the politics of the TVEI.' *In* Gleeson, D. (Ed) (1987) *op. cit.*

McGurk, H. (1987) *What Next: An Introduction to Research on Young People*. London, ESRC.

Meyer, J. (1977) 'The effects of education as an institution.' *AJS*, 83,1.

Midgley, S. (1987) 'British youth racist and disaffected with society.' *The Independent*, 3 December.

Moore, R. (1983) 'Further education, pedagogy and production.' *In* Gleeson, D. (1983) *op. cit.*

(1987)' Education and the Ideology of Production.' *British Journal of Sociology of Education* Vol. 8. No. 2.

Moos, M. (1982) 'Voluntary coercion.' *Schooling and Culture*. 12.

(1983) 'The training myth.' *In* Gleeson, D. (1983) *op.cit.*

(1984) 'How far further for further education?' *Youth Policy*, Vol. 2. No. 1

Morrison, P. (1983) 'Report on BBC Radio 4 interview.' Quoted by Jackson, M. (1983) 'Forces rally against political ban.' *Times Educational Supplement*, 23 September.

MSC (1977) *Instructional Guide to Social and Life Skills*. MSC.

(1981) *A New Training Initiative: An Agenda for Action*. Dec. London, MSC.

(1982a) *A New Training Initiative: Task Group Report*. London, MSC.

(1982b) *Guidelines on Content and Standards in YTS*. London, MSC.

(1983) *A Handbook for Managing Agents in YTS*. London, MSC.

(1984) *Notes of Guidance, Occupational Training Families*. (Bowyer and Sanzen) June 1984. London, MSC.

(1985a) *TVEI Review 1984*. London, MSC.

(1985b) *TVEI National Pupil Teacher Database Figs*. London, MSC.

(1986a) *TVEI Review 1985*. London, MSC.

(1986b) *TVEI: Progress Report on the 16–18 Phase*. NSG/86/11. London, MSC.

Nash, I. (1987) 'With No Place to Spare,' and 'No Place to Hide.' *Times Educational Supplement*, 13 November.

Newell, R. (1982) 'A smokescreen over the dole queue.' *Guardian*, 12 October.

Newman, G. (1985) 'Modules in TVEI.' *Times Educational Supplement*, 29 November.

Newsom Report (1963) *Half our Future*. London, HMSO.

NFER (1985) *The Management of TVEI*. Sheffield, MSC.

(1987) *The TVEI Experience: Views from Teachers and Students*. Sheffield, MSC.

NTI (1981a) *A New Training Initiative: A Consultative Document*. May, London, DES/MSC.

(1981b) *A New Training Initiative: An Agenda for Action*. Dec., London, DES/MSC.

Offe, C. (1967) *Industry and Inequality*. London, Edward Arnold.

Owen, J. (1984) 'TVEI: future control.' *In* Dancy, J. (1984) *op. cit.*

Pavett, D. (1986) 'The Joint Board and CPVE.' *Forum*, Vol. 29 No.1 Autumn.

Prais, S.J. (1981) 'Vocational qualifications of the labour force in Britain and Germany.' *National Institute Economic Review*, 98. November.

Prais, S.J. and Wagner, K. (1985) 'Schooling standards in England and Germany.' *National Institute Economic Review*, 112.

Pring, R. (1985) 'A form of life.' *Times Educational Supplement*, 14 June.

(1985) 'In defence of TVEI.' *Forum*, 27 (3).

(1987) 'The curriculum and the new vocationalism.' *B. Journal of Education and Work*, Vol. 1. No. 3.

Radnor, H., Ball, S. and Burrell, D. (1986) *The Certificate of Prevocational Education: An analysis of Curriculum conflict in policy and practice*. Paper presented at BERA Annual Conference. University of Bristol. Policy and Practice in Contemporary State Education.

Raffe, D. (1979) 'The alternative route reconsidered.' *Sociology*, Vol. 13.

(1983a) 'The end of the alternative route: the changing relation of part-time education to work life mobility of young male workers.' *In* Gleeson, D. (1983) *op. cit.*

(1983b) 'Education and unemployment: does YOP make a difference, and will YTS?' *In* Gleeson, D. (1983) *op. cit.*

(1987) 'Youth unemployment in the U.K. 1979–1984.' *In* Brown, P. and Ashton, D. N. (1987) *op. cit.*

Raffe, D. and Smith, P. (1986) *Young People's Attitudes to the YTS: The First Two Years*. Edinburgh, Centre for Educational Sociology, University of Edinburgh.

Ranson, S., Taylor, M. and Brighouse, T. (1986) *The Revolution in Education and Training*. Harlow, Longman.

Reeder, D. (1981) 'A recurring debate: education and industry.' *In* Dale, R. *et. al* (1981) *op. cit.*

Reynolds, D. *et al.* (1987) *The Comprehensive Experiment*. New York, Falmer Press.

Roberts, H. and Kirby, R. (1985) 'YB on YTS: why not?' *Youth and Policy*.

Roberts, K. (1984) *School Leavers and Their Prospects*. Oxford, Oxford University Press.

Roberts, N. (1987) 'Progression from CPVE: fact or fiction?' *SERCH* (Sheffield Ed. Research, Current Highlights) Sheffield, Sheffield University.

Robinson, E. (1968) *The New Polytechnics: A Radical Policy for Higher Education*. Harmondsworth, Penguin.

Rose, M. and Jones, B. (1985) 'Management strategy and trade union responses in work organisation schemes at establishment level.' *In* Knights, D. *et al.* (1985) *op. cit.*

Ross, K. (1987) 'Training for Equality.' *New Society*, 6 November.

Rustin, M. (1983) 'A right to work.' *New Statesman*, 4 February.

Rutter, M. *et al.* (1979) *Fifteen Thousand Hours: Secondary Schools and their Effect on Children*. Shepton Mallet, Somerset, Open Books.

Ryan, P. (1984) 'The new training initiative after two years.' *Lloyds Bank Review* No.152. April.

Sammons, P. (1983) 'Pattern of participation in vocational further education: a study of school leavers.' *In* Gleeson, D. (1983) *op. cit.*

Saunders, M. (1985) *Emerging Issues in TVEI Implementation*. Document of the University of Lancaster TVEI Evaluation Programme.

(1986) 'TVEI – a tiger, by the tail?' *Business Education*, November.

(1987) 'At work in TVEI: students' perceptions of their work experience.' *In* Gleeson, D. (Ed) (1987) *op. cit.*

Scruton, R., Ellis-Jones, A. and O'Keeffe, D. (1985) *Education and Indoctrination*. London, Educational Research Centre.

Seale, C. (1983) *FEU and MSC: two curricular philosophies and their implications for YTS*. London, Garnett College of HE.

(1984) *Some Trends in YTS Curriculum Theory*. Unpublished Thesis. London, Garnett College of Higher Education.

Senker, P. (1986) 'The TVEI and UK economic performance – an initial assessment.' *Journal of Ed. Policy*, Vol. 1. No. 4.

Shilling, C. (1987) 'Implementing the contract: front-line teachers in the TVEI classroom.' *In* Gleeson, D. (Ed) (1987) *op. cit.*

Siggers, T. (1987) *Better Schools? On the influence of TVEI and TRIST at the local level: a case study*. MEd Dissertation, Keele, University of Keele.

Skeggs, B. (1986) *Young Women and Further Education: A Case Study of Young Women's Experience of Caring Courses in a Local College*. (Unpublished) PhD Thesis. Education Department. Keele, University of Keele.

Smith, D.G. (1986) *TVEI – The School to College Transition: A Case Study*. MEd Dissertation. Keele, University of Keele.

(1986) 'TVEI replication and FE.' *NATFE Journal*, December .

Socialist Society (1983) The Youth Training Scheme: A strategy for the Labour movement. *Socialist Society*.

Stokes, P. (1987) 'The challenge of managing technical and vocational curricula in schools.' *School Organisation*, Vol. 7. No. 1.

TES (1986) 'Drop-out rates underline patchy effect of TVEI'. *Times Educational Supplement*, 31 January.

(1986) 'Fewer stay on as YTS recruiting takes off.' *Times Educational Supplement*, 6 June.

(1986) 'Carry on, TVEI/Young takes over vocational exams/Ten year programme to extend TVEI.' *Times Educational Supplement*, 4 July.

TURC (1985) 'Unequal opportunities: racial discrimination and the YTS.' *TURC*, October.

Taylor, C. (1988) 'Climbing towards a skilful revolution.' *Times Educational Supplement*. 22 January.

Tebbitt, N. (1983) *Conservative Party National Conference*. Brighton, Conservative Annual Conference.

Tenné, R. (1987) *TVEI Students: Three Years On.* London, MSC/TVEI Unit.

Thurow, L. (1975) *Generating Inequality.* New York, Basic Books.

Tipton, B. (1973) *Conflict and Change in a Technical College.* London, Hutchinson Educational.

  (1983) 'The quality of training and the design of work.' In Gleeson, D. (1983) *op. cit.*

Venables, E. (1967) *The Young Worker at College.* London, Faber and Faber.

Watts, A. (1983) 'Schools and the YTS.' *Times Educational Supplement*, 13 May.

Weiner, G. and Millman, V. (1987) 'Engendering equal opportunities: the case of TVEI.' *In* Gleeson, D. (Ed) (1987) *op. cit.*

Wellington, J. (1987) 'Stretching the point.' *Times Educational Supplement*, 25 December.

West Midlands YTS Research Project (1985) 'Unequal opportunities: racial discrimination and the YTS scheme.' Trade Union Resources Centre. Birmingham.

White, J. (1968) 'Instruction in obedience.' *New Society*, 2 May.

Whitty, G. (1982) Room to Move. *'Teaching London Kids 19'*.

Whitty, G. (1985) Sociology and School Knowledge. London, Methuen.

Wiener, M. (1981) *English Culture and the Decline of the Industrial Spirit 1850–1980.* Cambridge, Cambridge University Press.

Willis, P. (1977) *Learning to Labour.* London, Saxon House.

  (1984) 'Conclusion, theory and practice.' *In* Bates, I. *et al.* (1984) *Schooling for the Dole.* London, Macmillan.

Wragg, T. (1984) 'Evaluating TVEI Programmes:' In *TVEI Perspectives 14*. Exeter, University of Exeter.

Wringe, C. (1981) 'Education, schooling and the world of work.' *British Journal of Educational Studies* Vol XXIX, No.2, 1981.

Wyatt, H. (1985) 'TVEI and all that.' *Forum* 27 (3).

Young, M.F.D. (1971) *Knowledge and Control.* Basingstoke, Collier Macmillan.

Name Index

Ainley, P., 45, 49, 56
Anderson, D., 106
Ashton, D.N., 9
Atkins, M.J., 75
Atkinson, P., 29, 48, 52, 75, 106, 111
Avis, J., 31

Ball, S., 59, 60, 69
Barnes, D., 84, 85
Bates, I., 30, 47, 50, 80
Benn, C., 21, 46
Benson, G., 23, 104, 117
Bernstein, B., 59, 60, 70, 103
Blackman, S., 5, 9, 10, 48, 100
Blunden, G., 29
Bowes, A., 72
Brighouse, T., 89
Bristow, A.J., 20, 22
Broady, D., 53
Brown, C., 29
Brown, P., 9
Burgess, T., 18
Burrell, D., 59, 60, 69

Callaghan, J., 6, 47, 54, 56
Cantor, L., 18, 20, 22
Casson, M., 109
Cathcart, H., 50
Chitty, C., 80, 83
Clough, E., 24

Cockburn, C., 28, 46, 48
Cohen, P., 60, 73, 109
Collins, R., 47

Dale, R., 4, 56, 64, 80, 85
Dancy, J., 80
Davies, B., 83, 91
Dex, S., 30
Dickinson, H., 75
Durkheim, E., 49

Eggleston, J., 90
Erben, M., 75
Esland, G., 50
Evans, J., 83, 91

Fairley, J., 21, 46
Felton, D., 26
Fenton, I., 29
Finn, D., 4, 30, 47, 85, 105, 109
Fowler, G., 83
Freshwater, M.R., 52

Galloway, M., 112
Gibb, V., 29
Gleeson, D., 4, 6, 11, 22, 23, 27, 29, 30,
    31, 35, 40, 42, 47, 48, 52, 57, 80, 81,
    89, 90, 93, 100, 102, 108
Golby, G., 83, 91
Gorbutt, D., 83

Gorringe, R., 34
Grahl, J., 21, 46
Gray, J., 24
Green, A., 11, 33, 39, 72, 103

Hargreaves, D., 47, 87, 112
Harland, J., 9, 116
Harrison, M., 85
Hayes, C., 21, 23, 46, 51, 53
Hoare, Q., 109
Holt, M., 50, 57, 114
Hopkins, M., 35, 40, 42
Hordley, I., 22
Horne, J., 115
Horton, C., 25
Hudson, S., 25

Jackson, P., 114
James, E., 87
Jamieson, I., 10
Jenkins, R., 25
Johnson, R., 111
Jones, B., 24, 107

Kirby, R., 25
Knights, D., 103

Lansley, S., 23, 104, 117
Lee, D., 47, 50
Lee, G., 29, 48
Lee, J., 22
Lempert, W., 48
Lenhardt, G., 49
Lewis, I., 87
Lewis, P., 25

Mardle, G., 4, 22, 23, 40, 42, 108
Marsland, D., 45, 56, 57
Maunders, A., 6, 81, 89, 102
McCabe, C., 92, 93, 96
McCulloch, G., 3, 88, 89, 117
McGurk, H., 105
Meyer, J., 48, 111
Midgley, S., 105
Millman, V., 84
Moore, R., 50, 53
Moos, M., 21, 23, 46, 47
Morrison, P., 54

Newman, G., 87

Offe, C., 47, 49
Owen, J., 89

Pavett, D., 61

Prais, S.J., 76
Pring, R., 5, 52, 69, 82, 115, 116

Radnor, H., 59, 60, 69
Raffe, D., 11, 22, 24, 25, 30, 50, 107
Ranson, S., 89
Reeder, D., 3, 80, 117
Rees, T., 29, 48
Reynolds, D., 112
Roberts, H., 25
Roberts, I., 18, 20, 22
Roberts, K., 4, 11, 13, 18, 22, 107
Roberts, N., 72
Robinson, E., 18, 20
Rose, M., 107
Ross, K., 28, 29
Rustin, M., 104
Rutter, M., 91
Ryan, P., 21, 46

Sammons, P., 30
Saunders, M., 85, 86, 88, 91
Scruton, R., 45
Seale, C., 52, 54, 55
Senker, P., 74
Shilling, C., 84
Siggers, T., 75
Skeggs, B., 29
Smith, D.G., 90, 93, 100, 102
Smith, P., 24, 25, 50

Taylor, C., 12, 13
Taylor, M., 89
Tebbitt, N., 53
Tenné, R., 79, 84, 85
Thurow, L., 47
Tipton, B., 13, 18, 22, 62, 69, 107, 108, 115

Venables, E., 18

Wagner, K., 76
Watts, A., 10, 21, 23
Weiner, G., 84
Wellington, J., 48, 57, 114
White, J., 32
Whitty, G., 52, 57, 106
Wiener, M., 3, 80
Willis, P., 87, 91, 114
Wrench, J., 29, 48
Wyatt, H., 83

Young, M.F.D., 32, 103, 117,

Subject Index

A Basis for Choice, 63, 64, 65
A New Training Initiative, 6, 12, 58, 60
ability
  range, 10
access, 14, 19, 111, 112
accreditation, 71, 86
active learning, 10, 33, 69, 111, 116
Adult Employment Training Programme, 4, 7
adult training, 15
age, 19, 72
ALE, 72
apprenticeship, 20, 29, 30, 62, 73
arts, 115
'A'/'S' Levels, 98, 111
aspects of CPVE, 72
Audit Commission, 34, 35, 36

BEC 58, 63, 67
Better Schools, 3, 10, 62, 69, 70, 74, 84, 97
Black Papers, 5, 10
British Movement, 105
B/TEC, 1, 2, 9, 14, 19, 20, 27, 40, 44, 58,
  59, 60, 61, 62, 63, 64, 65, 67, 68, 69,
  70, 72, 75, 77, 79, 80, 86, 88, 91
Burnham, 32

categorical funding, 77, 79, 83, 116
CEE, 63
Circular 10/65, 80

City and Guilds, 9, 20, 44, 58, 59, 62, 63,
  67, 72, 74, 77, 79, 86, 91
City Technology Colleges, 13, 70, 77, 89,
  112
Civil Service, 21
class, 19, 20, 27, 28, 72
Clause 28, 39, 117
Clause 81, 34
Community Industry Scheme, 15
Community Programme, 15, 26
  health services, 28
comprehensive education, 40, 62, 77,
  82, 83, 110, 111, 112
  comprehensivization, 80
Conservative Government, 5, 6, 7, 12,
  21, 23, 43, 44, 58, 64, 73, 74, 80, 105,
  117
  Conservative Training Policy, 108,
  116, 117
  Party Conference, 61
continuing education, 112
control, 13, 116
CPVE, 1, 2, 3, 4, 6, 9, 14, 19, 20, 27, 30,
  44, 58, 59, 60, 61, 62, 63, 64, 65, 66,
  67, 69, 70, 71, 72, 74, 77, 80, 86, 89,
  92, 97, 98, 100
Crowther Report, 9, 12, 18, 23, 61,
  62
CSE, 58, 110
curriculum

core, 64, 65, 69, 86
cross, 10, 62, 65, 69, 84, 116
national, 2, 3, 6, 7, 9, 10, 11, 23, 62, 69, 82, 87
negotiated, 87

Department of Employment, 6, 38, 45, 46, 51, 81
DES, 5, 6, 7, 9, 11, 17, 20, 21, 23, 28, 32, 37, 38, 46, 56, 58, 59, 77, 81, 87, 88
DHSS, 11, 113
Dungeons and Dragons, 73

Education Act
  1944, 35, 62
  1986, 117
  1988, 2, 3, 5, 7, 10, 14, 34, 35, 36, 49, 64, 70, 80, 97, 111
Employer
  led 108, 116
engineering guidelines, 68
enterprise, 10, 11, 61, 114
  Allowance Scheme, 15
  mini, 11
  private, 21, 50
equal opportunities, 28, 29, 60, 78, 83, 84, 116
ESRC, 105
ethnic minorities, 30
Examination Boards, 61

falling rolls, 71, 79, 87, 88, 90
F.E., 3, 4, 6, 7, 9, 11, 13, 14, 18, 19, 20, 21, 22, 23, 24, 25, 26, 28, 29, 30, 34, 48, 62, 67, 70, 91, 94, 97, 98, 104, 107, 111, 117
  enrolments, 16
FEU, 6, 51, 67, 72, 94, 100
Foundation Certificate in Pre-vocational Education, 59

GCE/GCSE, 9, 10, 19, 20, 22, 30, 37, 38, 40, 58, 59, 62, 63, 64, 65, 67, 79, 86, 98, 99, 110, 111
gender, 19, 20, 29, 30, 105
general employment services, 15
general studies, 67
geographical mobility, 15
government training policies, 19, 28, 47
Great Education Debate (1976–79), 3, 6, 23, 37, 47, 61, 63,
GRIST, 3
guidance, 24, 52, 78

Hadow, 58
Haslgrave Report, 67
Hillgate Group, 10, 105
HMI, 5, 32, 37, 43, 91, 105
humanities, 115

idealism, 11, 73
ILEA, 30, 109, 117
industrial relations, 108n
industry, 13, 21, 28, 62
  local, 22
  manufacturing, 11, 22, 73
  training boards, 73
INSET, 35, 64, 69, 85
Institute of Manpower Studies, 46

James Report, 87
Job Training Scheme, 25, 26
Joint Board, 58, 59, 63, 66, 68
Joseph, Sir Keith, 61, 105

Labour Government, 46
labour market, 11, 12, 19, 21, 23, 30, 45, 50, 62, 72, 73, 104, 110, 111
LAPP, 1, 4, 20, 44, 58, 59, 70
latin, 10
LEA, 3, 6, 21, 23, 32, 34, 35, 40, 64, 70, 78, 79, 80, 82, 83, 86, 88, 96, 101, 104
liberal education, 58
  studies, 115
London Enterprise Agency, 117

modular training, 44
MSC (Training Commission), 2, 5, 6, 7, 11, 15, 18, 20, 21, 23, 28, 29, 32, 33, 35, 40, 45, 48, 56, 58, 61, 64, 81, 82, 83, 87, 90, 97, 105, 106, 110, 111, 112, 113

NAFE, 6, 7, 9, 15, 18, 20, 21, 23, 27, 33, 35, 37, 42, 48, 51, 56, 64, 71, 110,
  enrolments 7, 8
NATFHE 36, 41
National Front, 105
National Service, 28
National Training Policy, 49
NCVQ, 1, 3, 7, 19, 20, 23, 27, 32, 38, 49, 62, 64, 69, 70, 89, 92, 97, 111
Newson, 4, 32, 58
New Right, 5, 56, 105, 111
NFER, 79, 84, 86, 91, 9
NSG, 90
NTI, 1, 3, 6, 11, 12, 14, 21, 26, 75, 103, 105

Nuffield, 58
NVQ, 97

Occupational Training Families, 44
opting out, 70, 86, 112
Outward Bound, 11

personal effectiveness, 52
political literacy, 105
pre-vocational education, 14, 58, 59, 61,
    63, 64, 65, 70, 71, 72, 73, 77, 105
profiling, 24, 65, 69, 79, 84, 86, 99
  student, 67
progression, 60, 69, 70, 71, 77, 78, 80,
    82, 86, 87, 95, 111
  progressivism, 77
  police powers, 108
  production, 108
  productivity, 108
  staying on, 90, 94, 111
Programme of Political Education, 105

QUANGO, 92

race, 19, 20, 29, 30, 72, 105
  racism, 105, 106
realism, 11, 27, 73, 74
records of achievement, 65, 67, 79, 99
Refuseniks, 12
Restart, 15
ROSLA, 4, 12, 80
Royal Society of Arts, 9, 20, 44, 58, 59,
    62, 63, 65, 67, 72, 75, 77, 79, 86
Ruskin, 6, 47, 54

Sainsburys, 32, 37
Schools Council, 6, 58
Scottish Leavers Study, 50
SEC, 64, 69
sheltered employment, 15
skills,
  enterprise, 113
  generic, 28, 31, 44
  ownership, 113
  social and life skills, 14, 49, 51, 52, 57,
    79
  transferable, 28, 44, 51, 74, 107
social sciences, 115
social security, 19, 25, 26, 42, 57, 108
  benefit, 25, 26
social studies, 51
sociology of education, 18
State of Training Policies, 18
STEPS, 15

TEC, 58, 63, 67
tertiary, 7, 96, 111, 112
TES, 10, 24, 32, 90, 112, 117
Training Commission *see* MSC
Training Employment Programme, 19,
    25, 26, 27, 28
Training for Jobs, 3, 14, 32, 34, 36, 38, 64,
    74, 97
training policy, 6, 12, 13, 21, 26
Trent Polytechnic TVEI data base, 79
tripartism, 11, 14, 18, 30, 71, 83, 89, 103,
    115
TSAS, 97
TVEI, 1, 2, 3, 4, 5, 6, 9, 10, 14, 15, 19, 20,
    27, 30, 44, 58, 59, 60, 61, 62, 64, 65,
    67, 70, 71, 72, 75, 77, 78, 79, 80, 82,
    83, 84, 85, 86, 88, 89, 90, 91, 92, 93,
    96, 97, 98, 99, 100, 101, 104, 113, 116
TVEI Review, 82, 92, 96

Unified Vocational Preparation, 63, 88
unions, 23, 26, 104, 105, 108
  unionists, 21
University of Leeds National Evaluation
    Report (1987), 85

vocationalism, 50
Voluntary Projects Programme, 15

West Midlands YTS Research
    Project, 30
Wider Opportunities Programme, 26
work
  design, 108
  experience, 11, 24, 54, 60, 64, 78, 79,
    86, 87, 115
work shadowing, 11
working together, 3, 40, 97, 101
WRNAFE, 3, 97, 98

Young, Lord, 10, 76
youth labour markets, 7, 23, 31, 61, 80
Youth Opportunities Programme, 12,
    21, 23, 24, 63, 75, 88, 106
Youth Task Group Report, 46
youth unemployment, 18, 19, 20, 21,
    62, 104, 106, 116, 117
YTS, 1, 2, 3, 4, 5, 6, 7, 8, 9, 12, 15, 19, 20,
    22, 23, 25, 26, 27, 28, 29, 30, 31, 32,
    33, 38, 40, 45, 50, 53, 54, 59, 62, 63,
    64, 67, 70, 71, 72, 75, 77, 80, 83, 86,
    88, 89, 92, 97, 100, 104, 105, 113, 116,
    117